Christmas 1965

Mom & Dad,
        We hope you'll really
enjoy this excellent book.
Let us know — if you
like it we'll send you
the sequel.

                We love you,
                Joe & Joyce

I marvel that He would descend
from His throne divine
To rescue a soul so rebellious
and proud as mine.

A SOUL SO REBELLIOUS

Mary Frances Sturlaugson

Deseret Book Company
Salt Lake City, Utah
1981

©1980 Deseret Book Company
All rights reserved
Printed in the United States of America

No part of this book may be reproduced in any
form or by any means without permission in writing
from the publisher, Deseret Book Company,
P.O. Box 30178, Salt Lake City, Utah 84130

ISBN 0-87747-841-4
Library of Congress Catalog Card Number 80-69271

First printing October 1980
Second printing December 1980
Third printing January 1981
Fourth printing March 1981
Fifth printing June 1981
Sixth printing November 1981
Seventh printing June 1985

To my mother

Acknowledgments

I gratefully acknowledge the Glen Ellis family, the John
Strong family, Debbie Peterson and family, Grandma Reeder,
the Dinkleman family, Willie and Utahna Wilson, the
Boyack family, Clara Logan, Renee Vorhaus, the Mortensen
family , and many, many other families and friends who
helped make me a better me.

Contents

1

Reflections

I wish I could find that my sitting on this plane is all a dream. I would like to talk to someone and tell what it's all been like. But the lady next to me is resting her head against the seat and has her eyes closed.

I've always been a talker rather than a writer. In fact, Mama always said I talked too much, too often, and too open. I can still recall the constant "child, hush yo' mouth. Even the angels in heaven tire at hearin' yous run off so." But with all due respect to Mama, I'm going to try to express my feelings in the written word.

My name is Mary Frances Sturlaugson. I am black. I am a woman. I am a Mormon, and I am returning from a mission for The Church of Jesus Christ of Latter-day Saints.

Long before I had known any missionaries, my Mama had tried to tell me about the Lord. As I recall those times, I feel ashamed for the attitude I had toward the Lord. But though I felt I hated God many times, I also felt that somewhere deep within me I had believed in him.

Once Daddy found out I had stolen a bag of rice and gave me a beating for it. Afterwards Mama talked to me about how the devil would get me for being bad, but if I never did it again the Lord would forgive me. I knew that you had to be baptized to be forgiven, so a few days following that incident, during a cold rainstorm in late January, I went outside and stood in the pouring rain until I was completely soaked. I then asked the Lord to forgive me since I was now baptized. That night I landed in the hospital with pneumonia. I don't know how long it was before the fever broke, but I do recall waking and seeing Mama sitting by my bed. I remember asking her if the Lord had forgiven me. Mama dropped her head but not before I saw the tears in her eyes. "Child, you's been fo'given. Jus' git well is all yo' Mama want fo' you." I hadn't realized at the time how close I had come to dying.

I was born in Chattanooga, Tennessee, to Frank and Corine Sturlaugson. My birth caused no great excitement in the Sturlaugson household, for I was the fifteenth child, and another baby had become quite routine. They did tell me, though, that it was a cold wintry night, and I came screaming into the world with the help of a midwife, an anxious father, a very tired mother, and fourteen curious siblings. The event was of such note that in all the excitement no one bothered to record my arrival, and to this day there is no birth certificate to declare the truth that I do indeed exist. Nor was I to be the last child. Mama gave birth to eight boys and one girl after me, a total of twenty-four children.

As might be imagined, we were poor — very poor. We knew what poverty was all about. Our home was a small four-

room clapboard house in the Alton Park area of North Chattanooga. Our neighborhood was known as a ghetto, but to
me it was home.

Although we were poor, we were proud, and Daddy
would rather that we all starve to death than accept welfare.
Daddy was a good man and a hard worker. He would take
on work doing just about anything a person of our race was
allowed to do. He would sweep floors, carry out groceries,
collect pop bottles, do yard work, or any odd job that might
come his way. In fact, he would do whatever it took to
provide for us. He had only a second grade education, so
it was next to impossible for him to make ends meet. He
loved us all and we loved him. He taught us a lot of lessons
throughout the years.

There were days when we had almost nothing to eat
and we made ourselves sick by drinking too much water to
try to fill the empty hunger inside. Mama and Daddy would
gather us together and tell us stories of their youth to take our
minds off the gnawing hunger pangs until we fell asleep.
Occasionally Daddy would find an old television set and bring
it home. If we were lucky it might last a week. But even
though this served to distract us and fill our evenings, it made
me aware that I was different. I recall looking at TV and seeing
always the face of a white man behind all those things that
were great and beautiful. I began to think and wonder, where
do I fit in? What about my color? Why were we poor and had
nothing, and yet the whites seemed to have everything? I
began to feel quite worthless and even to hate my parents,
thinking that if they had not been black, then I would have
been a different color, white maybe, and I would have had the
good things in life.

At an early age I learned to steal—not for fun, but for

survival, and not just for myself, but mostly for my family. I also learned to lie — but that was for my personal survival. Lying protected me from the beatings that were sure to come from Daddy when I was caught stealing. Whenever I stole a bag of beans or rice from the store, I'd punch holes in it or rub it on the ground so the bag would look very unwanted. Then I would explain to my family that the grocer was going to throw it away, and because I happened to be there I had asked if I could have it. If my daddy knew any of us children were stealing, he would have beat us "white and blue."

We knew hunger and we knew persecution. But it was persecution more than anything else that caused us to grow up angry — angry for all the insults and injustices that were heaped on our race. I didn't realize how angry I had become until one occasion when Mama and I went shopping at the white ghetto. (We always referred to downtown as the white ghetto.) Mama needed some mending supplies, so we went to the five-and-dime. We stood at the check-out counter and waited while the young white girl decided whether or not she would help, as she put it, a couple of niggers. After some time she did finally get around to waiting on us. When the salesgirl totaled the items, Mama was surprised to find that they cost more than she had. She tried to explain that she hadn't realized she had gotten so much and offered to put some of the items back. The girl put all the items in a sack, saying it was "too late for that."

Mama dropped her head and gathered what small change she had in hopes it would cover the cost. At this point I snatched the paper bag from the girl's hand and said, "Which ones don't you want, Mama?" I had had enough! I glared at the girl, daring her to say a single word. I'll never forget that feeling — the blood coursing through my veins and the desire to beat her until she couldn't breathe anymore. Oh, how I hated her! Her face flushed dark red, but she didn't utter a sound. We left all the goods and went outside.

When we were out of the store Mama slapped me and told me how disgraced she was at how I had acted. I told her she shouldn't let people push her around. She was twice the age of that girl, and yet she let her step all over her as though she was a child merely because the girl was white folk.

As the tears came to Mama's eyes I realized she really felt hurt for the way she was treated. I knew she felt ashamed to have us children see her treated in this manner. At times like this Mama expressed to us her love for God. It seemed as though she centered her life around trying to please him. She would talk about God and how we should forgive others. To her a love for God seemed to sustain her in hard times or difficult situations. This always made me marvel, and I hated God for the suffering he caused Mama.

When she began to preach, the anger welled up inside of me again and I cried, "Oh, Mama, how long will you keep turning the other cheek before you realize it don't do you any good?" But Mama was a very staunch Southern Baptist, and she insisted that we attend weekly meetings and offer nightly supplications to the Almighty. This was gospel in our home. She taught us of a kind and loving God who does for all his children. Yet it seemed to me that in our circumstances, God had not done much. Despite all my religious training, I began to hate him. I wondered how Mama could teach me about a God who was loving and kind when so much of the opposite was happening to me.

Even though I was only nine at that time, I felt that I had seen and experienced much more than most nine-year-olds. I vividly remember the middle sixties when I was growing up —

the signs that said "for whites only," the times we rode in the back of the buses, the times we waited for whites to be served before our people could even get attention. I was too young to know why I had to suffer because of my color, but not too young to be hurt by hearing the words *nigger* or *coon* or *tar baby* or any of many other degrading terms.

At first I just cried when I heard white people call me those names. But then I heard of an idea called "civil rights." Black men in leadership positions in their communities were calling for a new generation of equal rights for blacks. There seemed to me to be two schools of thought on the subject of civil rights. One was represented by the Reverend Martin Luther King, a Southern Baptist minister. Mama liked the things he stood for, primarily change through peaceful demonstration and prayers to God. The other approach was advocated by Stokely Carmichael and his new united front — a coalition called "Black Power."

I was certainly in favor of improved conditions for blacks. The idea of equal rights seemed to me to be long overdue, even though I had been around only a short while — a fact Mama painfully pointed out to me every time I thought I knew a little something on the subject. I did not share her feelings, particularly since Dr. King was always saying that God would provide. I had just one question: where was God before Dr. King? I found myself more excited about the Black Power people. Yet, I felt depressed and angry the day Dr. King was assassinated — depressed because he could no longer champion our cause, angry because it was a white man who ended his dream.

This was a time of great frustration and uncertainty. I was frightened for the future. How was I going to meet the future as a black woman in a world of angry whites?

One night when I was twelve, about five of us children were home and Mama had just given us one of her stern lectures about "live an' let live, an' try an' get along." This was followed by one of her sermonette prayers to God. Almost always after these prayers Daddy would say that he was sure she had "done tired out the Lord with all her moanin' and groanin'."

Her lecture made me angry, because as usual she had reminded us that we were black and should stay in our place. Then she topped this with a prayer of thanks! Thanks for what? For a moment I could feel the heat rise in my body and my face flush red. It was then that one of my older brothers, Ernie, took me aside and for the first time I heard the words "Black is beautiful!" How good that sounded!

For several hours we talked, and I developed a new pride in my black skin. Stokely Carmichael had a new convert. I felt as though I could now singlehandedly whip any white man. There was only one catch. I was a girl, and Ernie told me that fighting was for men and the menfolk would protect us. I was left to battle with my best resource — my mouth. I took Ernie at his word. My mouth got my brothers into more fights than I like to remember.

The sixties passed and the seventies were far less violent than the sixties had been. The white man seemed to show a greater tolerance for blacks in general. But there were still "hot spots" of prejudice, particularly in the South. I still hated the white man and all he stood for.

By the time I was fifteen we had heard of a group of whites in our area that called themselves Mormons. Occasionally my older brothers brought home all sorts of stories about the beliefs of these people concerning blacks. I was sure the Mormons were secretly plotting to destroy all the "niggers" and send us back to Africa. My brothers told me that Mormons traveled together in pairs and dressed in white shirts. I thought if they wore white shirts in daylight, they probably wore white sheets in moonlight. I was almost certain they were in some way affiliated with the Ku Klux Klan.

I probably never would have paid much attention to them as a people had it not been for their teachings about the blacks. I was told that no black man could ever be anything in their church, and that they taught we were a cursed race. It really angered me and it hurt to think that any religion could teach these things. We had heard that the Mormons claimed that they were the true church of God, and yet it seemed to me they considered blacks the lowest human form. I wondered — if God was no respecter of persons, as Mama had taught us, how could they call themselves the true church and hold to such teachings? This was all I needed to hear about Mormons. I decided I could never be a part of any such organization or worship a God who taught those things.

Often as a family we would discuss the Mormons and other groups we considered racist. During these times Daddy pointed out to Mama and the rest of us that we had to stand up for ourselves, because if we didn't, we wouldn't find too many people who would.

It was on just such a night that I decided for myself that what Daddy said was true. I for one was determined to stick up for myself at all costs and to be fearless no matter what situations I might encounter. I had learned that when the soul is consumed with bitterness and anger, it is easy to be fearless.

A year passed and the long arm of the civil rights movement found its way into the heart of our ghetto. Federal laws were being enforced to see that all people had equal educational opportunities. A widespread system of busing was set up, and created quite a stir in both the black and white communities.

I attended an all-black high school. During my senior year, a time when busing was in full effect, I noticed that blacks were being bused into white areas, but no whites were being bused into ours. So I and a lot of other blacks refused to be bused. We were proud. We wanted nothing to do with the white world. We felt that what we had was just as good as what they had. If they didn't seek anything from us, we weren't about to seek from them.

During the first day of enrollment, news quickly spread through the halls that a white student was enrolling. Excitement was high because this was an opportunity for us blacks to show how much we hated whites.

The white student's name was Doug, and I was surprised to find that he was in my English class. There was never a time when Doug came to class and found a seat but someone would walk up to him and say, "Hey man, you're sitting in my seat." Doug would quietly apologize and move to a different chair. A few minutes later, another black would come along and say, "Hey, what are you doing in my seat?" Again Doug would apologize and move. Actually, seats weren't assigned to anyone, but this was the fun we had with whitey. There were times when I waited until close to the end of class and then turned to someone and told him that Doug was sitting in my seat. I relished the harassment Doug took. Again Doug would apologize and move. The teacher never said a word.

I kept waiting for the day when Doug would not come back. I kept thinking, "Surely, he's had enough." But day after day he returned. To this day I don't know why Doug went through all that he did. He wasn't being forced to come to our school.

Each day that Doug went to the cafeteria to eat became a treat for me. I had always wanted to be a great softball pitcher, and Doug became my practice target. I would take my bread and roll up a piece of meat or some potatoes in it, anything to make it soggy, and aim for the center of Doug's neck with a good, firm softball throw. If it hit him dead center, everyone would cheer me on. If it happened to splatter onto his head or his back, then everyone would just laugh. Doug would quietly wipe the food from his neck and finish his food and leave. Day after day he went through this.

Football season got under way. The cheerleaders were out on the field practicing when I looked up to see the team running out onto the field. I could not believe my eyes. I stood in amazement. There at the end of the line was Doug. We stared for a few seconds, then I looked at the other cheerleaders and said, "That honky has got to be crazy."

Football is a contact sport—for Doug it was mostly contact and little sport. I watched his teammates tackle him unmercifully. There were times when I would just stand still for fear he was dead. But time and time again he picked himself up and went right back into practice.

Doug didn't play in any of the games that season except one. That particular game happened to be against another all-black school and our biggest rival, Riverside High. When I looked up and saw Doug going into the game, I was shocked. Here we were losing, and the coach was putting Doug in! We would *never* have been able to live down the humiliation that other blacks would heap on us if we tried to win the game with a whitey on the field. The crowd finally picked up on what I was yelling at the coach — "get that honky off the field" — and they joined in. It must have looked as though the crowd and cheerleaders were about to start a riot against their own coach.

There's no doubt that the coach heard us, but he ignored us and left Doug in the game.

I've watched a lot of football games since that one, but I've never seen anyone play as hard a game as Doug played. He gave everything he could muster up for his coach, teammates, and student body; for a crowd and a school that had given him nothing but humiliation and pain. There was no doubt in anyone's mind that day that it was because of that one white player that we won.

At the end of the game I rushed out onto the field to try to congratulate Doug for the victory he had just brought us, but it was impossible for me to reach him. His teammates already had him up in the air, tears of joy streaming down their faces. At that moment, as I watched Doug up in the air, he wasn't the honky, the whitey, and all the other names we had chosen to call him. He was simply Doug, a teammate who had brought the team to victory.

I wish I could say things changed for Doug after that, but they didn't. Come Monday morning the joy of the victory was still in the air, but Doug was still white. We went back to our old ways.

At the end of the school year we had a community athletic assembly. A black named Michael received the "best player of the year" award. Michael was a strong, bright individual. He was a leader. When Michael told a joke we laughed and laughed, even if it wasn't funny. When Michael received his award, he thanked his family for giving him life and for supporting him through his childhood. He thanked his teachers for the knowledge they had given him and all the things that they had put up with. Of course, he told a few jokes and we laughed, even though they weren't very funny.

Then Michael became quiet. With his head down, he

stood there for what seemed like hours, and when he looked up again, tears were flowing down his face. The audience grew quiet, and shock hung in the air. This wasn't like Michael; he was a strong, unemotional fellow. When he finally found words he murmured an apology to the people who had chosen him player of the year. He went on to explain if they really wanted to pick a winner, they ought to have picked Doug. And then he briefly explained some of the things Doug had gone through that year. I thought the things I had done were cruel, but they were mild compared to what others had done.

Michael continued, saying that he wasn't a winner, but that Doug was. He said that Doug had endured more in a year than he would have been able to endure in a lifetime. With shoulders drooped, he went over and presented his trophy to Doug. They embraced, tears flowing down each face. The audience was completely silent.

For the first time in my life the thought occurred to me that someone white could be human.

2

It's a Long, Long Way

My senior year in high school seemed to go by faster than any of the other years, and when time for graduation came, I felt empty and somewhat sad. I really liked school, and it didn't seem quite right to me that it should already be over. There was a gnawing uncertainty about the future. Just the thought of leaving old friends and familiar routines made me uncomfortable, and I tried not to think about what lay ahead.

Sometimes during our school days Daddy had kept us home to help him with odd jobs. He would send us to white neighborhoods to collect pop bottles or to find scrap metal to sell for enough money to buy food. Sometimes we went to the local corn silos, where Daddy had us gather the kernels that had fallen to the floors. That was hard work and I hated it. However, Mama took what we brought home and made hominy and grits, our favorite treat. To us hominy was like steak. Though the work provided food for our bellies, the thought of grubbing for scraps in white backyards was degrading, and I gave Daddy all sorts of excuses as to why I had to be in school. This more than any other reason is why I learned to love school.

Daddy knew that school was important. He often said he wished he had had more schooling. All he could do was print his name, and we had to read and write his mail for him. It was painful for him to be so uneducated, and often he would tell the boys that he wished he had had the same chance for schooling that they had. Yet he also knew that a family had to be fed, so education or no, the work came first and we all had to help.

If Daddy wanted me to work and I wanted to go to school, I would begin to press him for permission to go to school. The answer was always no, but I would persist. If all the excuses brought no result, I would run off in tears. This, in and of itself, was never enough to persuade Daddy, so every few minutes I would send my little brother Johnny back to tell him that I was still crying. Daddy would let me carry on sometimes for more than an hour, but eventually his heart would soften and in his deep gruff voice he would holler, "Okay, fool! Go on then, starve to death. Yo' Mama's sick, the babe ain't got no milk, and you just sittin' there thinkin' of none other than yous self." Then he would turn and walk off, leaving me sitting in silence while all my brothers and sisters stared at me accusingly.

I would feel very guilty—until I was out of the house and on my way to school. Then I would tell myself that it was all worth it. Anything was better than what I was sure Daddy had in mind for us. I made up my mind each day that

I was going to learn something new and worthwhile that would benefit me or my family. And I always did.

It was a beautiful spring day late in May when Mama, Daddy, brothers, sisters, aunts, uncles, and cousins all gathered at the Howard High School auditorium to see the family's first high school graduate. There were nearly five hundred students in our class and I, an honor student, had a part on the program. Mama was so proud, and I thought at any moment Daddy was going to stand up and shout "that's my daughter" as I gave my presentation. I was hoping that he recalled all the times I had cried to go to school, and that he was thinking to himself that it was all worth it. I felt proud to think that I had accomplished something no one else in my family had done.

Mama made me a new dress for the occasion. I had no idea she was making it until the hour before it was time to leave for graduation. She came into my room carrying a package. I had been crying because I wanted to look especially nice for my part on the program, and I knew I had nothing nice to wear. I also knew we were too poor to afford a luxury such as a new or even a secondhand dress. Mama handed me the package, a neatly wrapped grocery sack tied with a thread. She watched as I anxiously untied it and said sweetly, "Child, the Lord do truly provide." Inside was a plain white cotton dress trimmed with inexpensive lace. Down the front was a row of red buttons I knew she had cut off one of her own dresses to add a little color.

I was dumbfounded, and all I could say was, "Oh, Mama!" I was excited, yet I felt a twinge of guilt for my selfishness. I marveled that Mama would do this for me. She had no sewing machine, so I knew the dress had been made by hand. She didn't even own a thimble, and I could see the prick marks in her thumb where she had forced the needle through the material. I couldn't find the words, but my swollen eyes gave her the message — "I love you, Mama." Tears began to roll down her cheeks. She turned away quickly and scolded gently, "Child, now yous better hurry on 'n git yo'self ready else yous gonna miss yo' own gragashun." Mama could never quite pronounce graduation.

That day seemed to be the apex of my life. No one could ever again say I was a "dumb nigger." I had an education. I would never have to pick up another pop bottle.

Now that high school was over, most of my friends were looking for work, but not me. I was smart — or at least I thought I was. After all, I had graduated with honors and was only seventeen years old. I wanted more high points in my life, so I decided to go to college — not just the local city college but a real institution of higher learning, complete with on-campus housing. In my neighborhood it was unheard of for a girl to go anywhere but our own black McKenzie College, but I wanted to go far away and challenge the outside world.

Mama was both scared and proud that her baby girl should decide to go on to college. She was scared for me because of my poor attitude toward whites and my disregard for the ways of the Lord. She felt sure these attitudes would lead me into trouble. I'm sure she even thought I might wind up dead so far from home. But she was proud of the things I had accomplished, and it gave her no small pleasure to tell the neighbors that she was going to be the Mama of a college girl.

On the other hand, Daddy spent the entire summer fretting over how they were ever going to pay for a girl in school while there were still mouths to feed at home.

I worried too about paying for any further education, so

in the summer I took work at the Milk Bucket, a local ghetto drive-in just up the block from our house. The job paid $2.30 an hour, minimum wage, and I worked full time for the next two months. I would have worked longer, but Daddy made me quit the night the store was robbed.

Most of the money I made went to the family. It seemed they always needed something and, of course, there was always an emergency. It made me feel wonderful to be able to help them even though I had only a small amount left for school. I wondered how I was ever going to make it. It was already the end of July and I had not heard anything from the schools I had written to.

During the last part of my senior year I had made application to several colleges that I thought might accept me and provide full scholarship as well. My only hope to attend college was a full scholarship.

One of the schools to which I applied was Tennessee A & I, an all-black, four-year university in Nashville whose main purpose was to allow blacks the opportunity of furthering their education. I felt reasonably confident they would accept me because of my high grades. My high school counselors had suggested that this state school offered the best opportunity for a full scholarship.

The other two schools to which I applied were ones that I knew very little about and were chosen at random. One was a small college somewhere in Missouri, and I no longer even remember its name or where it was. The other college was Dakota Wesleyan University in Mitchell, South Dakota. I chose this school because it was located close to two Indian reservations and I assumed there would be a predominantly Indian student body. The idea of studying and living among the Indians intrigued me, and I wanted very much to study

their culture and do social work among them. I admit my
ideas about Indians were somewhat distorted, as I had learned
them from the few television westerns I had seen. I felt that
the Indians were a horribly oppressed people in servitude to
the whites, and I truly empathized with their situation. I had
never seen a real live Indian, and I was anxious to see one
for myself.

The days of August dragged on, and daily I waited to
hear that I had been accepted at one of these schools. I spent
the days close to home to be first to get the mail. Each day
began with mounting anxiety and anticipation, but when the
mail brought no reply I would become depressed and doubt
that I would ever have the chance to go to college. My family
shared my disappointment but saw no reason for me to fret.
I resented their efforts to console me, and I shut everybody
out so I could wallow in self pity.

I began to despise our poverty even more. Why were we
so poor that there was not enough money to help me realize
my ambitions? I was also impatient. Daily Mama asked God in
her prayers to somehow provide a way for her baby girl. She
never doubted for a minute that somehow the Lord would
work things out. I wondered how she could possibly cash in
her faith for enough greenbacks to see me through college
when we couldn't even put shoes on our feet or sufficient food
in our mouths.

One day in the middle of August, several days after I had
decided that I would never get an answer, word came.
Among the bills was a formal, white envelope addressed to
Mary Sturlaugson. It was the first piece of real mail I had ever
received, and I didn't even mind that it was in a *white* envelope. My hands shook as I tore open the letter. I was fearful
that the letter would say my application had been rejected or

that I could come only if I could finance my own way. It didn't say any of those things. I began to read it again, this time more carefully. I read the heading — old English type emblazoned with a seal — that said Dakota Wesleyan University. I went on. The letter said that after careful review the acceptance committee had approved my application for enrollment. It stated further that because of my high scholastic average, SAT scores, ethnic background, and financial situation, I was to be awarded the Jubilee scholarship. This scholarship provided full support contingent upon my maintaining a 3.0 grade-point average and would be renewable for subsequent semesters for the duration of my college career as long as I met the standard outlined.

I read the letter over and over in disbelief. By this time the family had gathered around me, and Mama kept prodding me to read the letter out loud. I suddenly realized what had happened. At first I cried, then I laughed, and then I shouted for joy. I read the letter aloud. Mama's eyes filled with tears as she stood by my side in a near stupor of disbelief at what she was hearing. I can't even remember everything that was said, but I do recall Mama's words above all the rest, "Thank the good Lord!" Over and over she repeated it. Then she turned and went to her room, shutting the door behind her. I knew exactly what she was doing — she was on her knees.

During the days that followed there was only one topic of conversation in the Sturlaugson household — my going to college. My brothers and sisters all spent time at the library trying to find out about South Dakota, while Daddy just tried to learn how to pronounce the name of the school. Mama was scared for me to be going so far from home, and in my heart I too was afraid of going away. South Dakota sounded so foreign to me. However, I never openly admitted it.

A few days after the initial letter of acceptance I received a large manila envelope filled with pamphlets, information, and forms for me to sign. I could hardly believe that it was all happening, and I began looking forward to school with a spirit of adventure.

The remaining days of summer flew by, and I thought the day of departure would arrive before I could accomplish all that I needed to do. School started the first of September, but freshman orientation was held during the last three days of August. That didn't leave me much time.

It didn't take long for the news to spread through the ghetto that I was going to a university in South Dakota. Daddy worried about how I was going to get to school, but family, friends, and community all pulled together to raise what they could. Small donations came to the house daily. Even little old ladies would stop me in the street and give me fifty cents or a quarter.

The extra money that came to us was a great relief to Daddy. His health was beginning to fail, and he was limited in what he had been able to do. It seemed to all of us in those weeks prior to my departure that he was no longer himself. He lacked energy and was plagued continually by a racking cough that left his whole body weak. He spent many hours in quiet contemplation. It wasn't like him to act this way. I often wondered if these spells of solitude were because he was sick or because he was sad at the thought of my leaving. I noticed too that he didn't seem to have much appetite. Mama always fixed him a plate at suppertime, but for days at a time his food was left untouched. This upset Mama, and she was after him constantly to eat something. In just a few short weeks my father's giant frame seemed to wither and grow old. The stern but loving countenance and his strong, handsome face gave way to hollowed cheeks and glazed eyes.

Mama knew something was wrong and urged Daddy to go to a doctor. Daddy just laughed and said, "Woman, t'aint nothin' wrong wif me. 'Sides, doctors always just a takin' people's money 'n t'aint doin' no good anyhows." I'm sure Daddy was thinking that any money used for a doctor would have to come from my school money, and he wouldn't allow that.

Finally the morning came for me to go. I hadn't slept very well the night before. All I could think of was the excitement of going to school, the fear of the unknown, and the sadness I felt at leaving home. I loved my family very much, and I knew I would miss them. It was 4:00 A.M. when Mama woke me to say it was time for me to go. It was dark outside, and through the broken window I could smell the fog still heavy in the air. Daddy was already up and working to get our old green '59 Ford pickup started. In the cool early morning air I hurried to get ready. I put on my best dress and the new shoes my brothers had bought especially for me. They wanted me to look nice while I traveled and also when I got to my new school. I was no sooner dressed than my brothers Roy and Charles tiptoed into the room to carry out the old battered trunk that housed all my worldly possessions. The younger children were up by then, and I said a fond and tearful goodbye to them.

Outside, the truck was loaded and the engine running. Daddy, Mama, and I climbed into the front seat and Roy, Charles, and Johnnie jumped in the back. It took nearly twenty-five minutes to get to the bus station, and I felt sure I would start to cry before we all got there. I thought of the little ones at home and how they all cried as I said goodbye. Next

to me Daddy was solemn, but Mama sniffled the entire way. I
wished she would stop. She wasn't making it any easier.

At the bus station Daddy asked Mama and the boys to
wait while I went with him to buy a ticket to Mitchell, South
Dakota. The man behind the glass figured out the cost and
made small talk while he wrote the ticket. He seemed surprised that someone my age was traveling alone all the way
to South Dakota. Daddy then pulled out his money pouch
to pay the man, and I counted out the proper amount. We
were surprised to find we had a surplus of about fifteen
dollars. This extra bit of money Daddy folded in my hand and
told me to keep it for myself. He was so proud of me.

The announcement to board the bus was made, and I
clung desperately to those last few moments with my family.
I gave each one a hug, and by this time the tears flowed freely.
I really loved those boys, and I knew I would miss them as
much as they would miss me. Mama, between sobs, tried to
give me last-minute instructions, and Daddy spent his time
trying to console Mama. I put my arms around Daddy, and he
held me close for a long time. When I looked up he was
crying, and I knew somehow that I would never see him
again. Then I turned and hugged Mama.

Daddy reviewed the bus route with me one more time to
be sure I had it right. I assured him I did, and then I climbed
aboard the bus. As I got to the top step my brothers called
out to me. I turned around and there they stood—all three
with their fists raised in salute to black power. Mama scolded
them, and we all laughed. I turned, took a seat by the
window, and watched them all until the bus pulled out.

The trip took all that day, all that night, and all the next
day. The hours seemed long, and the sights that at first intrigued me gave way to routine. I was left to my own wits to

keep me entertained. I read the information I had received from the university over and over. I read it while I munched on the teacakes Mama had given me earlier that morning. It didn't surprise me to find a faded picture of Jesus tucked under the teacakes. It was so like Mama to do something like that, and I laughed to myself as I thought of her. I knew she was concerned, and I'm sure this was her idea of a gentle reminder. I stared at the picture for a long time and then offered a silent prayer.

Dear God, bless Mama and take care of her, and dear God, watch over Daddy and his cough. I love them and miss them. And also God, bless me, because, you see, I'm going to miss them all, and I'm just a little scared at this idea of going away. I surely would appreciate it. Amen.

Mama believed in prayer, and I knew she would be glad at my offering one. It was more for her sake that I prayed, as I didn't take much stock in religion myself.

Small towns and large cities came and then were gone. Every horizon took me farther from home, and with each mile I missed my family more and more. I thought about my dear sweet Mama and Daddy and all the children. I thought about the good times, our old house and its broken furniture, the neighborhood where I grew up, and the friends I had left behind. Although I knew people could see I was crying, I wasn't ashamed. I loved and missed my family and didn't care who knew it.

Deepening Trials

Mitchell, South Dakota, was a big surprise. The farther I got out west, the fewer black people I saw. By the time I arrived in the state of South Dakota, I saw absolutely no black people at all. I found myself constantly stared at. I grew more and more disappointed and apprehensive. My only consolation was seeing real live Indians. Each time I saw one I was totally fascinated, and I longed to share these experiences with my family.

It was a rather humid day when the bus arrived in Mitchell, and the humidity made me homesick. It wasn't until I got off the bus that I realized I didn't know where the campus was nor how I was to get there. As I stepped off the bus I was greeted by a white hand, followed by a voice explaining who he was and why he was there. My fear was soon replaced by anger. The white man was the football coach. He had come to pick me up along with a few football players. I turned to see three big young men standing nearby. They also were white!

I looked first at the coach's hand and then into his eyes and said coldly, "Thanks, but no thanks." Then, very slowly and distinctly, I told him my daddy did not approve of my being in the company of whites and neither did I. I told him curtly I would rather walk.

The hot, humid air must have hit him hard at that moment, because his face went from pale white to cherry red as beads of sweat poured from his forehead. The three players cut short their conversation and stood by with their mouths open as if waiting to be fed. The coach explained that the college president had asked him to pick me up and give me a ride to the dorm. He also went on to tell me it was too far to walk with luggage. I still refused to ride.

We all stood there in silence, and I was sure that under his breath he was calling me a few of the choice names that white people reserve for blacks. He asked if I wanted the president to come get me. "White's still white," I told him, "and I'm not riding with no honky." I then walked to the phone to look up the number for taxi service. I still had the money Daddy had given me, and I knew he would rather have me use it for a cab than be dependent on the white folk for anything.

The coach explained that there was no cab service available. Angry and frustrated, I rode with him to the campus. I was glad my family and our community couldn't see me. My family would have been the laughing stock of the whole ghetto. I could see the neighbors pointing fingers and saying, "Already your daughter has become an Aunt Jemima." (An Aunt Jemima is the same as an Uncle Tom, and nobody likes Uncle Tom except the white man.) The ride was stifling. The coach tried to make conversation, but I sat unresponsive. The three players in the back had not uttered a word since my comments at the bus depot. It surely was the longest ride I have ever taken, though it took less than ten minutes. I can't imagine how long it must have seemed for the coach.

The car stopped in front of a three-story red brick building, and the coach announced that this was the dormitory where I would be staying. Without a word I got out, followed by two of the young men in the back. They began taking my trunk out. At that moment an elderly white woman opened the door and gave me a cheery welcome. I turned to the coach and asked if the whole place was made up of people "their" color and where were the black and Indian dorms. "I surely don't want to live around you white folks," I told him very sarcastically.

The coach sounded rather irritated as he told me the whole school was "their" color. I rudely replied, "Oh brother, that is all I need, a bunch of stinking whites." Then I walked past the lady to a phone booth I'd spotted in the lobby. Once inside, I looked back at the five of them. The coach was explaining something to the woman, who stood with a frown of disbelief on her face. I picked up the phone, knowing I had no one to call. My family did not have a phone and neither did any of the neighbors. Realizing that the coach and the others were still watching me, I pretended to be talking to the operator and then to Daddy. I ended the false conversation rather loudly with "Okay, Daddy, just get me out of this salt mill."

All were silent when I walked back out. I boldly asked the woman where my room was. The coach told the young men to take my trunk up, but I told them not to touch it, that

I would take it up myself. "It's up to you," the coach said as he walked away yelling "good luck" to the woman.

I lay on my bed for what seemed like hours. The room was nice and large. The bed was a good one but felt uncomfortable. I had been used to a mattress stuffed with odds and ends to fill the holes that had worn into it over the years. I gave the mattress a hard press trying to feel the springs, but my hand met with only a soft resistance. At home I had often awakened to find the spring wires embedded in my body. Most of us kids were scarred from being scratched by them.

I had arrived a day before incoming freshmen were scheduled to arrive, so I was the only one in the dorm. The dorm mother, the woman who had greeted me so cheerily, phoned to see if I would like to have dinner with her, since the school cafeteria wasn't open yet. I told her no and hung up with a bang. Now my body ached with hunger pains. I had tried the old water trick, but it only left me vomiting dry air and with greater pain. I longed for one of Mama's biscuits with thick, rich flour gravy. Thoughts of Mama made me homesick. The hunger and the loneliness doubled up on me as I cried myself to sleep. My last thoughts before I fell asleep were of the ghetto and wondering if I could really make it on my own.

Throughout the next day more girls arrived. There were still no other black students — and no Indians either. Several times I walked to the bathroom, sometimes for no reason except to let them know I was there. When spoken to I would look them in the eyes and continue walking, not responding. Around one o'clock my door opened. A girl asked if I were Mary, and before I could answer, she rushed over and gave me a hug and told me that she was going to be my roommate.

I pushed her away rudely as if she had a contagious disease, and without a word I walked out of the room. Without knocking, I walked into the dorm mother's room. Using the explicit, ungodly words my brothers had taught me, I told her to get that honky out of my room. The language brought her hand first to her mouth and then to her heart as fear came to her face. Swearing, I turned and walked out. I really wanted to be a college girl and make my family proud of me, but I didn't want to be in the atmosphere of the white man. Whites were my enemies.

The next few days went both fast and slow — fast as far as getting oriented to the campus, but slow in my adjustment to the white person always being around. At least I had the privacy of my own room. The president had talked to me about the roommate situation. Due to a shortage of students he allowed me to room alone, but if enrollment went up in winter, I was to have a roommate.

He asked why I didn't want a roommate. In no uncertain terms and in very graphic language I told him my feelings for whites. He spoke like Mama about learning to get along, but I made it clear to him that I didn't need the white man's friendship in order to learn. I was here to get a college education, and who I got along with should not be his concern. He was worried because he wanted love on his campus — without that love there could be no real togetherness. I'm sure he left feeling that there could never be any togetherness between me and him, nor between me and the whites.

My feelings of resentment deepened. Why hadn't the white people thought about love and togetherness years ago instead of treating us like animals? It hadn't mattered if I was good or bad; just being black was all they had needed to dismiss me as a worthless nigger. No, the whites had better not ever give me that "trying to get along" line when it was they who had practiced just the opposite.

My hatred definitely gave me added strength as I went from day to day. I always picked a table away from everyone else at mealtimes. The food wasn't the greatest. It definitely wasn't soul food! Often I'd take the food back up to the server and tell her to feed it to her mama, because she probably wouldn't know the difference between it and dog food. If the shower water was cold, I'd swear and say, "Dumb, stupid, inconsiderate white trash." My regular physical education soccer class was cut to one and a half weeks when the teacher realized I was out for blood. I felt obsessed with hatred. Everything about the whites seemed to irritate me, and my soul felt like a brick wall. There were days when I'd simply walk around telling myself that white people didn't exist, that I was simply living through a nightmare.

My teachers grew to hate the hour for my classes with them. I was constantly on the defensive, always waiting to hear something that sounded like a derogatory remark about my people. When I thought I heard such a remark, I would tear into that person, not caring if I humiliated him or her.

One of my teachers made the mistake of saying that whites had higher IQs than blacks. Before I could say a word a white student spoke out. "That's a bunch of bull," he said. Then he asked the teacher how much she knew about black culture or conditions in the black areas. By the time he finished there was very little I could say. I looked at the student and then at the teacher and said, "If I took you to the ghetto and gave you an IQ test, your IQ level would not be as high as that of the average muskrat. And they can't read, they just smell." The class roared with laughter, though I meant the statement seriously.

I never could understand the white man's way of justi-
fying his intelligence. It always seemed a one-sided scale to
me. My daddy didn't have a textbook education, but he was
smart with a knowledge of life. He not only knew how to survive himself, but also to see to it that his family survived as
well. He knew how to establish a happy home, one filled with
love despite our many problems. Daddy knew the importance
of a father to a family; he didn't take off when the times were
rough. And most of the times had been rough. My daddy had
"smarts," and I was proud of him for his intelligence and
knowledge — knowledge that hadn't come from a textbook.

Many of the whites tried to break down the barrier of
hatred that I had built up, but I made it clear that it was there
to stay. I didn't like whites and would never change. As my
brothers had always said, "You can never trust a honky;
he'll laugh to your face and stab you in the back."

I had gone to South Dakota thinking I was smart, but
the first day of class made me realize just how far behind the
average white student I was in my education. The textbooks
the whites had handed down to us after they were finished
with them had not been one or two years old but more like
five or ten. In order to maintain the necessary grade-point
average, I not only had to keep up with the other students,
but also catch up on education I had missed. Realizing how far
behind I was in my education created greater bitterness for the
white man. If we had had the proper textbooks, I would not
have had to struggle so. I felt it was another way of holding
us back and then calling us "dumb niggers" when we couldn't
pass the same tests.

My social life was spent doing things alone. Boys would
call me for dates or have different girls try to get me to go on
blind dates, but I would just say they weren't my kind. One

night a boy called and said, "Nigger, you think you're too good to go out with whites." I hesitated before answering, feeling sure he knew I would give a smart answer, but I simply said "Yes," and hung up the phone.

I worked at two jobs on the college work-study program. I saved or used half the money I earned for necessities and sent the rest home. Daddy's health had really deteriorated, and he was constantly in and out of the hospital (in because Mama made him go; out because he would sneak away each time). Because of his health Daddy had set up a system for survival. Each of us children was responsible for one of the younger ones. We had to support him or her as if they were our own child. We also had to contribute something, even if it was only a quarter, to a family account. Daddy was trying to make sure his family would be able to carry on in case death took him from us. We readily supported the system Daddy established, and I know it made him proud to see his family beginning to prosper. I took whatever money I didn't send home and went shopping. I would buy something for myself, something for Bobby, the brother I was supporting, and something special for Mama and Daddy. Or, since we now had a telephone, I would call home.

I often went to movies, though I believed them to be tools of racism. A heart can bear only so much, and mine had borne all it could the night I went to see the movie *Easy Rider*. The movie was about two motorcyclists riding through the South. As usual there was a put-down scene, and naturally it was pointed at the black people. Roars of laughter filled the theater. I sat there feeling the blood rush through my veins, angry at the way everyone was laughing at my people. I waited until the laughter stopped and, feeling like a giant, rose to my feet. Using the choicest words of my ungodlike vocabulary, I called them as many names as I could think of. I told them that only a bunch of sick people could get their "jollies" from humiliating another race of people.

When I sat down my whole body was shaking, not with fear but with anger. I waited for some "redneck" to make a comment, but no one said a word. I know I could have lost my life that night, but I also know that I would have fought for it with my last breath. I remembered Daddy saying, "We have to stand up for who we are, because if we don't, we won't find too many who will do it for us."

What happened that night was quite an eye-opener. Later on during the movie, there were some more scenes ridiculing blacks, and they were funny, yet no one laughed. I wondered as I walked home that night, why can't people always be considerate of the feelings of others?

During the year I tried out for cheerleading, knowing that if I won it would have to be strictly on ability and not popularity. The cheerleaders were supposedly chosen by the student body, but usually only the athletic teams voted. I knew that they had only one name for me, "Stuck-up Nigger."

There weren't the usual whistling and teasing when I did my two cheers. I heard only one real low whistle, and that one was very faint. We all did jumps and followed that by singing the school song. Everyone joined in, and as we stood there singing, I started to laugh. Before me were hundreds of whites. The funny thing was that they all looked alike. I suppose it surprised them to see me laughing, because they had never seen me laugh. Not knowing why I was laughing, some of them began laughing too.

When I went to my room after dinner a large banner hung on my door with the word "CONGRATULATIONS." I had been elected cheerleader! I opened my door and on my desk was a bouquet of flowers — not one dozen flowers but two dozen or more. There was also a card that read, "Congratulations, Mary. We are proud to have you as a cheerleader." It was signed "The Athletic Teams." At that moment I really don't think I could feel anything. An hour or so later, I wrote two thank-you notes and placed one on my door and one on the coach's door.

That night I called my family and told them all that had happened. Mama cried and told me that the young people had to be the ones to change this world. She further explained that I had to learn to love white people and that the good Lord would take care of those who did me wrong. Daddy told me not to take any wooden nickels — his way of saying "Be careful." My brother Roy told me to make sure I didn't marry a white, or my brothers would hang us both. There was the usual good feeling as we all said goodbye, but something was different. I think Mama felt hope, Daddy felt uncertainty, and my brothers felt fear — fear that their baby sister would be brainwashed and lose the full meaning behind black power. They had no reason to fear. Although lots had happened to me, my feelings for the white man had not changed.

Cheerleading was fun even though the team was white. Whenever we played a school that had a black player, I would cheer for him. My loyalty went to my race first and my school second. The cheerleaders and players never said a word about it.

When I did not have classes or was not at work or cheering, I spent time writing my family long letters. I knew Mama worried about me and my attitude toward whites and God. I gave Mama a hard time about God and love, but I still marveled at the strength she had. I felt she could carry the weight of the world on her shoulders and yet never utter one complaining word. Mama was strong and kind, and I was very proud of her. I didn't want her to worry, so I wrote lies to her that I was attending one of the local white churches.

Later I was elected homecoming queen. It was an honor but also a disappointment. The homecoming king was white. He and I had to ride in the homecoming parade together, and that brought me no joy. I suppose I am the only home-coming queen to ever ride through a crowd of friendly faces and waving hands without smiling. I waved half-heartedly every so often.

Later I competed in a preliminary contest to select a representative for the Miss South Dakota pageant. I will never forget how degraded I felt toward the end of that pageant. I had not been acting like myself but someone else in order to win a crown. When I was selected as one of the five finalists, I knew I had to be me in order to salvage my dignity. The judges gave me the question, "If you could be anyone for twenty-four hours, who would it be and why?"

I stood speechless for a moment, thinking of the many times in my childhood when I had gone hungry and cold; how I had gone to bed at night and dreamed of being rich and being able to buy lots of food, or of living in a warm home, not big and fancy but simply warm. I thought of the many times whites had yelled and called me nasty, ugly names that made me cry, and how I had wished I were some-one famous and beautiful. I felt a tremendous hatred for the many times I had been made to feel worthless. I answered the judges: "If I could be anyone for twenty-four hours, I would be my Mama. My Mama knows how to love whites when hatred comes so easy for me. My Mama knows how to reach out and forgive them when they do her wrong, while I would rather spit in their faces and walk away. But if I could be my Mama, it would not be to feel and know her goodness, but simply so I could go back and step on all the white people I have watched step on her just because she was black." I turned and went back to my seat. There was total and complete silence. Then I heard a few handclaps, followed by more, and then still more. I did not win the crown, and that came as no surprise. One lady came up to me afterwards and said, "Those judges couldn't accept a good honest answer, could they."

Mama sounded disappointed when I called and told her what had happened. Of course she gave me one of her sermons on learning to forgive and love. Mama never stopped trying!

4

Wonders to Perform

In the spring of that trying year at Dakota Wesleyan, I was offered a job on one of the Indian reservations. I was overjoyed at the opportunity to work with the Indian people. I found them to be just as curious about me as I was about them. Their curiosity was filled with love, and I did not feel like a stranger with them. Life on the reservation brought a lot of love and happy times into my life, things I had not felt since leaving home.

The Indian people taught me much about themselves that was totally contrary to the things television and even history books had taught me to believe. My love for them grew, especially for my Indian sister, Sarah, with whom I shared an apartment. Sarah and I had met when we worked together at the school on the reservation. I taught English to children who were junior high school age, and Sarah was a teacher's aide.

Sarah took great pride in teaching me about the history of the Indian people, a history filled with misfortune and mistreatment. She had a hatred for the white man as strong as my own, and it forged an automatic bond between us. We spent long hours at night discussing life and what we wanted the future to be like for us and our children. I told her that I felt that only hatred had enabled me to survive life this far, and about Mama and her love for God. Sarah and I shared the same feelings for God. We knew that if there were really a God, he had to be white, and he cared only about the white man.

Saturday afternoons were especially fun. Sarah and I usually had people over, and we would sit for hours listening to music while we gossiped. It was on such an afternoon that we were interrupted by uninvited guests. I heard a knock and went to look out through a small shade that covered a window on the door. I was surprised to see two Mormon missionaries standing outside our door. (Anyone who has lived on an Indian reservation knows that, in general, the only people who walk around in suits and ties are the Mormon missionaries.) I told everyone there were two Mormons at our door. My look of disbelief brought my friends to the window also. We stared out at the missionaries and then we began to laugh. Sarah did not like whites, and after hearing what the Mormons taught about blacks, she felt even less friendly toward Mormons. We all looked out again and laughed, repeating this action about six or seven times. The last time, as we looked out, the missionaries were staring at each other trying to see if one of them possibly had something on backwards.

Finally I decided to take the opportunity to let the Mormons know how I felt about them. Opening the door, I invited them in. Once they were inside I immediately started swearing at them for their teachings about my race. The missionaries stood looking confused and afraid, yet they did not offer a word of defense. Seeing that I wasn't going to get an argument out of them, I told them I would give them five minutes to explain, and that their explanation better be a good one.

I never thought that five minutes would extend to half an hour. When I realized that they had my attention with their explanation I became uneasy. I had never intended to listen to them. Quickly I told them to get out because they had overstayed their five-minute limit. They apologized for staying so long. They left us an invitation to attend church on Sunday. "I'll never attend your stinking church," I screamed as I slammed the door behind them.

Neither Sarah nor I attended church. Our Sundays were planned out in advance. We slept until noon, ate lunch, slept again until seven in the evening, watched *Kojak*, and then went back to bed until Monday morning.

On the Sunday following the visit of the two missionaries, I woke up early. I was puzzled as to why I had awakened so early. I could tell from the constant movement of Sarah's bed that she was awake also. We finally decided to fix breakfast, something we rarely did, especially not on Sundays. Even after stuffing ourselves with a big breakfast, we could not go back to sleep. Finally I said, "Oh Sarah, let's go." I didn't say where, but she immediately agreed and began dressing for church.

We arrived at the small Mormon chapel and were greeted by the two missionaries who had visited us the day before. They were all smiles. Because of the constant mentioning of Jesus Christ, I was quickly turned off by the meeting. Sarah soon asked if I felt we had had enough of hearing about God and I told her yes. We then got up and walked out, noticing the disappointed look on the faces of the missionaries.

We discovered that going to the Mormon church that Sunday had been a mistake. It became impossible to get rid of those two missionaries in the weeks and months that followed. They wanted to share a message with us, but we didn't want to listen. Day after day they returned with their message, and day after day we told them in no uncertain terms to get lost. When language failed to discourage them, we reverted to physical abuse. One day we called them on the phone and told them we were ready to listen and to come over early enough to have dinner. We then boiled some water and when they arrived, we opened the door and announced that dinner was over but that they might as well drink up. We threw the water on them, closed the door, and laughed. They still kept coming back.

At that time the missionaries were at the breaking point trying to teach me. Completely discouraged, they called the mission president to ask his advice. They told him about the black girl to whom they strongly felt they were to teach the gospel, but who refused to let them. The mission president asked them if there was a romantic interest. One of them briefly explained to the president some of the things I had done to them and then said, "Now tell me, president, could there possibly be a romantic interest?" The president reminded them of the Church's policy and told them not to go back anymore. But early the next morning, shortly after seven o'clock, he called them back and said, "Elders, I don't know why, but keep trying to teach her."

Months passed and the missionaries got nowhere in their efforts to teach me the gospel. One day as they stood knocking I opened the door to once again make threats on their lives. But of all the many times they had stood before me, I had never seen what I saw then. I saw love on those two faces. The words I had planned to say somehow came out this way: "Either you guys are crazy or I am, so come on in so I can be sure it's not me."

At first accepting the things they taught was hopeless because of the pictures they used. They showed me pictures of Joseph Smith and said he was a prophet for these latter days just like the prophets of the Bible. I didn't care about the Bible and its prophets nor did I care whether God had called a prophet to the earth in my lifetime. My suspicions that God was white and only cared about the white man were confirmed when I saw that God had called a white man to be prophet. The missionaries showed me a picture of twelve apostles, and they too were white. At this point I told them to get out and go teach their white racist ideas to someone else, because I didn't care to know about what white folk had been chosen to do this or that for "their" God. Bitterness welled up within me. Everything that was good or highly regarded always seemed to have a white man behind it.

The next day the missionaries returned and asked if they could please share their message with me, this time without showing me any pictures. So I told them, "You two are as bad as my Mama — she never gives up either."

We began to progress. Little by little I recognized feelings that were unusual for me, and little by little I became afraid. I tried to suppress these feelings with negative thoughts about Mormons and whites, but the feelings inside just wouldn't go away. I tried to define what they were but couldn't. All I knew was that my strong hatred of and bitterness against the Mormons were disintegrating.

I finally called Mama one night to talk about these feelings that I could not understand. When I heard her voice, all I could do was cry. Mama must have thought something serious had happened because she immediately put my brother Charles on the phone. I told him that I thought I was beginning to believe in a God. My brother was quiet as I sobbed heavily. After a few moments listening to me cry, he yelled to Mama to come to the phone. I heard him explain he thought I was losing my marbles and that I had better come back home.

I tried once again to tell Mama what I had told Charles, and, as I did, she started crying. "Child, the good Lord moves in mysterious ways; yo' mama been prayin' real hard for yous and is so happy that yous found the Lord."

I explained to Mama that the God I was talking about was the Mormon's God. "God is God of us all. Just be happy yous believe in him," she said. Mama also tried to explain that that strange feeling I was worried about was the love of God, but this I denied. I told her I didn't want any feelings of love for God. I could tell this hurt her, and later I felt bad, but I was being truthful.

Later Mama told my brothers that the Mormons had been talking to me about God. That night my brother Roy called me back. "Stay away from 'em," he told me sternly. "Who?" I asked. A cold lump of fear knotted my heart. I knew he was going to say the Mormons. "Those no-good Mormons who go around teaching that you are lower than the animals of this earth, that's who." I tried explaining but he refused to listen. More of my brothers got on the phone and, in general, gave me the same advice. Mormons were no good in their book and never would be.

Sarah too began to allow the missionaries' message into her life. At first we made jokes about their message, but gradually the jokes became fewer and fewer until we almost entirely stopped talking about the Mormons. We each were wrestling with new and unidentified feelings — feelings we just couldn't joke about.

The weeks that followed were nightmares. I had decided not to return to college that fall. I couldn't find contentment in anything. No matter how late I stayed up at night, sleep would not come. Food was tasteless. Music lost its appeal. Nothing seemed right. I finally refused to see the missionaries, thinking the frustration would go away. But that didn't work either. I felt downright miserable. This feeling was worse than the persecution I had experienced during my childhood. Then I had recognized the feelings as hatred, but now I didn't know what they were, and it was frightening.

I began to take long drives to secluded places on the reservation in hopes of escaping. Escaping what? I didn't know. Sometimes I sat and cried; other times I stared into space for hours. When I couldn't do either, I sat and talked out loud to myself about my family. I tried to relive some of the good times when we were all home together. Praying occurred to me often, but I refused to pray. I knew if I did it wouldn't be because Mama wanted me to; it would be because I was beginning to believe in God. I was not ready to accept that fact. The missionaries had even tried getting me to pray, but I just couldn't and wouldn't kneel down to a God I felt was white.

I stumbled out of bed one night swearing because I

wanted to sleep and couldn't. I slipped on a coat and house slippers and stepped outside. A fierce South Dakota blizzard hit me full force, but I continued to keep going. A strong gust of wind and snow knocked me to my knees, and as it did, I really didn't care at that moment if I died. The bitter cold wind and snow soon mixed with my tears as I remained there on my knees swearing at God. I screamed at him and told him to leave me alone. I didn't want to change. I wanted him to go away and leave me in my prison of darkness.

I sat crying, my whole body filled with hopelessness. A scripture the elders had read one night kept coming to my mind—"How long can rolling waters remain impure?" I shouted out loud to God, "Please let me know what you want. Mama said you loved me. If you do, let me know or please go away and leave me alone."

I owe my life to Sarah. She nearly died from the pneumonia that she contracted while searching for me that night. I escaped without even a cough.

In January I called my family to tell them I knew there was a God. I told them I believed the Mormons and the truth they taught about Jesus Christ. My brothers ended the conversation by giving me a choice — my family or the Mormons. My brother Johnny said if I joined the Mormons he would regret until the day he died that I had ever been born his sister. In every family there is always one to whom you feel closest, and for me it was Johnny. He couldn't have hurt me more at that moment if he had threatened to take my life.

Ernie, who was living in Chicago, called later that same night and he was furious. Until then he had ignored the news about my new religion and belief in God. He had thought that it was all a joke, especially since it involved the Mormons. He wanted me to deny that it was serious, but I said nothing.

He asked me if I wanted to be a rotten traitor to my race and to my family, and gave me one last chance to deny that everything was true. I wanted desperately to lie as I had done as a child, but I found that I couldn't. Ernie hung up calling me cruel names.

I was terrified in the days that followed. What if my family really deserted me? I would have no one, absolutely no one. My own family was hurting me, and the hurt was nearly unbearable. I thought about the many times I had hurt people and wondered if their pain had been similar to what I was now experiencing.

Sarah and I started having horrible nightmares at night. The apartment was filled with an evil feeling so real that we were afraid to be alone.

One night Sarah's screaming awakened me. I rushed over to her and turned on the light. She was halfway out of bed as if someone had been pulling her. She stared at me. I asked her twice what was wrong but she didn't say a word. Instead she remained sitting stiffly, glaring at me. Fear hit me hard. I'm still not sure if I said the words or someone else did, but I heard a command being given in the name of Jesus Christ for Satan to leave. I know my lips moved, but I had never heard or given such words before. Immediately after they were spoken Sarah slowly lay back down and continued sleeping.

Trembling, I went to the phone and called the elders. Elder Sekona answered on the first ring, and before I could tell him it was me, he said, "Mary, are you all right?"

Elder Sekona had awakened and felt an urgency to call Sarah and me, but, realizing how late it was, had decided not to. The feeling continued to be impressed upon his mind. He finally had gone to the bathroom to pray aloud for understanding and guidance. Midway through his prayer he found himself commanding Satan to depart from our presence. He had gone to the phone to call us when his own phone rang.

The elders gave us each a blessing of protection and strength so that we might understand and endure whatever adversities might befall us.

On January 31 I stood staring into the water of the baptismal font. I tried to comprehend all that had happened since the missionaries had begun teaching me. I also tried to understand why. I wondered if more was yet to come and if I would truly be provided the strength to endure. Yet I still felt a sweet sense of peace and comfort. The Lord knew I didn't have much faith. I had prayed to him just the night before and told him all the doubts and fears I had. I told him I had not reached the point where I honestly felt that Joseph Smith was a prophet, because Joseph Smith was white. I asked him to please give me a sure knowledge that this white man was indeed a prophet and that I would no longer doubt. I stayed on my knees for hours waiting for an answer, but nothing happened. All I got was a question: "What are you going to do with the few things I have given you a sure knowledge of?"

Now as I stood ready to be baptized, I knew I was still filled with doubt and very little faith. But as I had gotten up from my knees the night before, I had told Heavenly Father I was trusting my all in his hands even though my all wasn't much. Sarah had resolved her doubts too. Just as we had suffered through the uncertainty together, now together we had accepted the challenge to be baptized.

"Mary, what you are about to do is right, and please don't doubt that it is." I turned to see Elder Sekona standing next to me. As I stared at him with tears in my eyes, I had to smile and marvel at how he always seemed to know my thoughts. He had endured so much with me. After all the hardships I had put him through, never once did he show discouragement. Through all the cruel things I had done and said, he had always shown love and concern. At that moment I was deeply grateful for his persistence. Had he not kept trying, I would not know the God I had come to know.

A girl played the piano as people waited for the service to start. As I listened I began silently repeating the words to the song she was playing:

> *I stand all amazed at the love Jesus offers me,*
> *Confused at the grace that so fully he proffers me;*
> *I tremble to know that for me he was crucified,*
> *That for me, a sinner, he suffered, he bled and died.*
>
> *I marvel that he would descend from his throne divine*
> *To rescue a soul so rebellious and proud as mine;*
> *That he should extend his great love unto such as I,*
> *Sufficient to own, to redeem, and to justify.*
>
> *Oh it is wonderful that he should care for me,*
> *Enough to die for me!*
>   (*Hymns*, no. 80)

I really couldn't understand what I had done or could do that the Lord would want me. How could I ever be anything in his eyes?

Elder Sekona wiped the tears from my cheeks as he asked me if I doubted the Lord. "Elder Sekona, I love my family. Why does the Lord ask us to sacrifice the things or people we love the most?" Elder Sekona didn't answer me for a while; he just stared into my eyes. Then he said, "Mary, whatever sacrifice he asks of you, or me, or anyone, it's only for a small moment. And as he asks of us, he gives in return twofold. He will also grant unto us the strength to endure that sacrifice. He doesn't ask that a sacrifice be cruel — he loves us too much for that. We show him how much we love and trust him when we obey his commands. Mary, sacrificing your family hurts, but someday the joy will far outweigh the hurt you feel at this time. Remember the scripture that says that 'all things shall work together for thine own good.' Mary, they will."

The tears were still falling steadily as I stepped down into the waters to be baptized. "Happy?" Elder Sekona quietly asked me as he took my hand and led me into the waters. "Yes and no," I whispered to him. "Yes because I know it's right; no because I'm afraid you might drop me, and I can't swim!"

Shortly before Elder Sekona began the baptismal prayer I snapped my head to look past him. The movement had been so definite that he too looked, then asked me what was wrong. I shook my head to indicate nothing. I had the strangest feeling that someone was standing there watching us, but when I had turned to see who it was, no one was there. I felt sad not seeing anyone, but then a feeling of peace came. I knew my baptism was being witnessed by someone I couldn't see — someone who was very happy for me.

5

The Spirit Whispers

After I was baptized and confirmed a member of The Church of Jesus Christ of Latter-day Saints, I stood and bore my testimony. I can't recall exactly all that I said, but I do know that I thanked the missionaries for their love, patience, and endurance. I do remember stopping constantly to fight back the tears that kept choking me. At the end I said, "I know that difficult times still lie ahead of me, and I'm going to rely upon your love to pull me through. I appreciate the love and light each of you has given in your own special way to my life. I would like to ask one more favor of each of you. Will you please pray for my family? I love them very much, and it's hard knowing that I have had to make a choice between them and the gospel. It's the hardest thing God has asked of me." In closing I told them that I hoped that I too might be able to give to others the love and light they had given to me.

On March 26 of that same year Daddy died. I was told by my aunt that he suffered greatly. Daddy, who had weighed close to two hundred pounds, was eaten up by cancer. By the time he died, he weighed only fifty-four pounds.

No one bothered to call and tell me that Daddy had died. I was at the Indian high school that Friday morning when the Spirit quietly told me. At the moment the Spirit bore witness to me of his death, I was laughing and talking to the lady who worked in the school office. In the middle of a sentence I stopped, stared blankly at her, and said, "My Daddy has died." She seemed puzzled at first but then she rushed over to me and told me to sit down. Telling her I would be all right, I walked out and went home.

Sarah was home when I got there. She noticed right away that something was wrong and asked what had happened. After telling her, I called my sister in Chicago. I recall asking her, "When did Daddy die?" She was totally surprised and asked me how I knew he was dead. I didn't answer her, but repeated my question. She told me that *their* daddy had died on Wednesday, and they would be burying him that Sunday. She told me to stay away, that I had caused enough grief in the family, and not to cause more with my presence. She told me *their* daddy wouldn't want a Mormon at his funeral.

I'm not sure if Daddy knew about my being baptized a Mormon. He had been in the hospital during the times I had called home to tell my family about the Mormons. I often wondered if he had known if it would have made a difference to him. But even if it had, I don't think he would have allowed my brothers to treat me as they did. I didn't misunderstand my sister when she said *their* daddy, but I also didn't remind her that he was *our* daddy.

I asked Sarah what I should do about going or not going to Daddy's funeral. She answered very sternly, "Yes, we are going to *our* Daddy's funeral." Sarah and I had only two days to make it to Tennessee. When we arrived the funeral service had already started. As we walked into the church I honestly felt that my brothers were going to pick me up and throw me out. I didn't try talking to them. Sarah and I just sat by ourselves with the other people there.

As I sat through the ceremony, I realized I had lost not only my Daddy but my family, too. I felt really alone—the lowest I had ever felt.

I can still recall the deep ache I felt as I watched my Mama. She looked so tired and alone. It reminded me of the way she looked when I had tried to baptize myself in the rain and had nearly died. I longed to go put my arms around her and hold her close.

"Oh, Mama, I love you. Please let me help you through this," I cried in my heart. When Sarah put her arms around me and the lady next to me looked at me sadly, I knew I must have said the words aloud. As I watched Mama I noticed she wore the dress I had sent her for Christmas. I felt that she had known that my brothers hadn't told me about Daddy's death, so she wore the dress so something of mine would be a part of his funeral service.

When the service was over I stood back while everyone walked out. Mama was the only one of my family who looked at me as they passed. I tried to say I love you with my eyes, and I know Mama did the same in the quick glance we were able to share.

Sarah and I drove to the cemetery at the end of the service. I had planned to stay by Daddy's grave long after everyone else had gone, but my brothers saw me and came over to order me to leave. I didn't say a word. As I walked away from Daddy's grave, I remembered Doug and how he too had never answered when we persecuted him. Suddenly I understood how we reap what we sow.

I can't remember the two-day ride back to South Dakota. When we arrived home I went to the bedroom and closed the door. It grew dark as I sat there thinking about Daddy, but I didn't bother to turn on a light.

It's amazing all the things one thinks about when a loved one dies. My thoughts lingered on the many times Daddy had come home looking tired and beaten from working odd jobs to feed us. Yet it seemed that no matter how tired he was, he could always muster up a smile as he gathered us all together for a game of softball. We didn't have a real softball and bat, just a ball made of old rags and a bat made from the branch of a tree. We would play until late evening and then enjoy listening to Daddy tell us about his youth.

As I recalled the many memories I had of Daddy, I began to cry for the first time since I had known of his death. It just didn't seem fair for him to die. Loneliness and grief tore at my heart as I realized that I never once had told him verbally that I loved him. I had written it to him and Mama, and in other ways had tried to tell him, but I had never spoken the words directly to him.

I went to stand at the bedroom window. Looking up to the heavens I asked my Heavenly Father if he would let Daddy know that I loved him. "Heavenly Father, my brothers told my aunt that I caused most of Daddy's suffering. Please tell him I'm sorry. I never meant to if I did. Please tell him of my love."

I was still talking to Heavenly Father when the bedroom door opened slowly and Sarah came in. One of the missionaries wanted to talk to me. I don't recall which missionary it was, but I do remember that he talked to me about Daddy. He had me tell him all that I could remember about him. And then he sat and let me cry.

Before the missionaries left that night, we all knelt in prayer. I thought one of the missionaries would give the prayer, but they asked me to do so. I was grateful that they did, because while praying, I felt great peace. I knew that Daddy was no longer suffering with the pain of this life.

6

Encounters

Not long after Daddy died, the elders had me preparing to go to Utah. They felt it would be a good experience for me to be around the Saints in Utah—that the Saints there had a spirit and love that would help me gain greater strength.

I didn't realize how much I loved those missionaries until it was time for me to leave. Elder Sekona had been transferred a few days after my baptism to Minot, North Dakota, but the night before I left for Utah, he called me. He gave me lots of brotherly advice on keeping my testimony strong no matter what life brought my way.

Sarah rode with me to Mission, South Dakota, where she would be living for a while. There we said our goodbyes. We cried more than we talked. Sarah was truly like a flesh-and-blood sister to me. Later that evening as I prepared to write in my journal I found a note from Sarah. It was short, but it said everything: "Mary, a part of *me* will always be *you*; a part of *you* will always be *me*. This much is certain no matter what happens. Sis, I love you. Sarah."

The state of Utah was beautiful. The Indian Placement Service had arranged for me to live with a family in Provo until I was ready to be on my own. I felt both excited and scared. It was almost like the feeling I had when I first left Tennessee to go to South Dakota. Except this time I had what Mama had tried so long to lead me to — the Lord.

The Ellis family, with whom I lived, were beautiful people. Any fear I felt was quickly washed away upon meeting them. They radiated love and made it impossible for me to feel like a stranger. Dad Ellis greeted me at the door with a glowing smile and said, "Welcome home, Mary."

The weeks passed quickly, and I busied myself getting accustomed to my new life. I made lots of dumb mistakes, especially with the cherries of Utah. I soon discovered a hidden love for them and suffered frequent stomach pains from eating too many.

Adjusting to the people was easy after I adjusted to the many stares I got. I had to laugh the day I was out shopping and a little boy, seeing me, tugged at his mother and said, "There's a chocolate lady, Mom." His mother was embarrassed, but as I walked by I smiled, patted him on the head, and said, "Hi." He looked puzzled, probably because he had never heard "chocolate" talk before.

By the time summer came I had decided to take a couple of classes at Brigham Young University. It was heartwarming the way the students helped me find the different buildings where my classes were located. I marveled at how I never had to ask for directions. Whenever I stopped to look at my small map of the campus, someone would stop and ask me if

I needed help. When I told them where I was trying to go, they would proceed to walk me to the particular building and the specific classroom. The students really had a special love and concern. I always felt their willingness to help. Of course, I also got the usual stares.

One day I was taking an English test for a campus job when a young man walked into the room. The room was completely empty and he could have taken a seat anywhere, but he sat right next to me. I continued taking my test, though I wondered why he had chosen that particular seat. After a while I heard only the sound of my writing. I had not heard him turn a page or anything. Turning quickly, I looked to see what he was doing. He sat staring at me. I caught him by surprise, and he quickly looked down at the book before him. I turned back and continued working on my test.

Unable to really concentrate, I turned back to him and asked, "May I ask you a question?"

He rather enthusiastically said, "Sure." I then asked him why he had been staring at me.

"I was trying to think of something to say to you, but by the time I thought of something appropriate you turned and caught me looking at you and I forgot what I had planned to say," he answered very honestly.

"Why did you have to think of something to say?" I asked him.

"Well, I've never talked to a black person before and I didn't want to say the wrong thing. I was trying to make sure that what I said wouldn't come out all wrong." He smiled and shrugged his shoulders as I turned back to my test.

After my test was finished we sat and talked for hours. When we finally parted I asked him if it had been difficult talking to me. "No. I guess I should have remembered people

are people on the inside even though they may have a different skin color. Thanks Mary. I enjoyed our talk. Good
luck." And like the missionaries had always done, he reached
out his hand to shake mine.

Life was happy for me in Utah, but it was also difficult. I
was frequently disillusioned by the attitudes I saw in people,
especially the attitudes toward my race. Despite what the
Saints said and taught, that we were all brothers and sisters, I
still sensed that they thought I was different because I didn't
have all the blessings of the gospel that they had.

One night I went to see *Carousel*. In this particular pro-
duction a white man had been made up black to play one of
the characters. This "black" man was kicked out of heaven
and roamed the earth as a nuisance. The audience roared
constantly with laughter at his stupidity. I sat feeling not the
same bitterness and hatred I had felt when the people had
laughed at *Easy Rider*, but a deep hurt. I was close to tears.
I had to tell myself constantly not to cry, and I fought desperately to hold back the tears.

At the end of the play everyone but me stood to give the
cast a standing ovation. Several young men were sitting next
to me; one of them must have been aware of my silence
throughout most of the play, because at first he stood up but
then immediately sat back down. One of his friends leaned
over and asked why he wasn't standing. He quietly whispered
something back to him. His friend then whispered something
to the man next to him. Within seconds, all the young men sat
down. When the standing ovation was over, the young man
next to me leaned over and told me he was sorry. The tears I
had been holding back began to fall, and I quickly stood up
and left.

Outside I thought about what had just happened. I felt

a deep gratitude for the young men sitting next to me, especially the one who had apologized. He knew I had been hurt by the character in the play, and he felt sorry. Thinking about brotherly love, I felt close to him even though I didn't know his name. He was someone who knew the meaning of the pure love of Christ.

It took a while for me to get over that night and to face the fact that Mormons were human and capable of faults and mistakes, even though they had the gospel and its teachings in their lives, some even from birth.

One day Mom Ellis and I went shopping for materials to start my book of remembrance. While we shopped I questioned her about why I couldn't go through the temple, since I was female and females could not hold the priesthood anyway. She tried to explain, but I failed to understand — or perhaps I didn't want to.

When we arrived home I went straight to my room and closed the door. I sat for hours feeling resentful. It just didn't seem fair that my Heavenly Father refused me blessings because of the color of my skin. I found myself questioning my decision to join the Church. As I sat there the door to my room opened. Mom Ellis walked in, quietly placed a pillow on the floor, and suggested that I ask my Heavenly Father for understanding. After she left, I stood up and threw the pillow against the wall. I felt bitter toward the Lord, and I didn't want to pray to him because of what I felt was his total injustice.

I must have fallen asleep, because when I woke up it was dark outside and the house was still; apparently everyone had gone to bed. I stood up and got ready for bed in the dark. I thought of saying my prayers, but I refused to do it. I didn't have anything to say to such an unfair God. I closed my eyes and tried to sleep but I couldn't. The Lord simply refused to let me sleep until I listened to what he had to say. "Behold, I am Jesus Christ, the Son of God. I am the same that came unto mine own, and mine own received me not. I am the light which shineth in darkness, and the darkness comprehendeth it not. Verily, verily, I say unto you, if you desire a further witness, cast your mind upon the night that you cried unto me in your heart, that you might know concerning the truth of these things. Did I not speak peace to your mind concerning the matter? What greater witness can you have than from God? . . . Look unto me in every thought; doubt not, fear not. . . . Be faithful, keep my commandments, and ye shall inherit the kingdom of heaven." (D&C 6:21-23, 36-37.)

Hours later I still lay sobbing. Maybe I couldn't enter the temple, but there was still the greatest of all temples, that of my heavenly home, and that was the one I was to strive to enter.

A week after that experience I went to a park to relax and think. While there something else very interesting happened to me. I wrote it in my journal as a poem.

I was amazed at the small face that peeped
over my shoulders as I sat reading on the
cool, green earth.

"I love black," the child-like voice uttered,
as she wrapped her tiny arms around my neck.
I turned to smile into the shiny blue eyes
that showed so much love.

"What are you doing?" were harsh words that
interrupted what I was about to say.

I turned to see a lady approaching.
Rudely, she pulled the child away.

"I told you to stay away from those people,"
she continued as they quickly walked away.
I looked to see the little helpless form wave a tiny hand
*   of goodbye*
and the eyes reflected lack of understanding.

Tears formed in my eyes, and quietly I whispered,
not sure if it was a question, "I am a child of God."
I looked again at the tiny form almost lost from view.
"Blessed are the pure in heart, for they shall see God."

I realized then that I would always be confronted with obstacles in this life, but I had to be as strong and loving as a child.

I finally bore my testimony in church one Sunday. It was the fourth of July in the bicentennial year — two hundred years of freedom! At first I wasn't going to bear my testimony, but toward the end of the service I found myself unable to remain in my seat. At first I stumbled for words, but then the words came tumbling out.

"My brothers and sisters, I wasn't sure if I should bear my testimony because of the hurt and resentment I've felt this day. All around me people have spoken of 'freedom.' People's faces glow with the joy they feel for that freedom, but I don't know or feel that joy. I don't really feel a part of the freedom this country celebrates although I was born and raised here in America. My forefathers' blood and sweat helped build this country; yet America has made me feel as though I don't belong here. I've noticed how many other races of people come to this country and are made welcome, but I'm left to feel worthless.

"But that's all right, because I do have a joy inside me, and that's the joy of the gospel of Jesus Christ. It's a joy that no man can take from me. It's a joy that makes me feel loved and wanted each and every second of the day. Many times people look at me and frown or say unkind things simply because of the color of my skin. It's at times like these that my Father in heaven reaches out and puts his arms around me and gives me a fatherly squeeze full of love, full of forgiveness, and full of strength to go on.

"I want each of you to know that I don't just know *about* my Father in heaven, I *know* him. Just as I love my Father in heaven, I have that same love for each of you. I may not know you each personally, but simply knowing that we all share the same Father in heaven is enough. I pray that someday we will truly come to love each other the way our Father loves us and wants us to love each other."

7

O That I Were an Angel

Who said "There is nothing permanent except change"? My life thus far had been a study in change and contrasts — hatred melted by love, strong family ties suddenly severed, punishing poverty to comfortable, secure circumstances. Truly my life could be painted in black and white in more ways than one.

But in spite of the warm glow of happiness I had found when I embraced the gospel, there yet seemed to be an emptiness inside me and nothing could fill it. I yearned to fill a mission. I spent a lot of time speaking at sacrament meetings and firesides, and I felt good in this service, but I wanted to be in service to the Lord full time. I wanted to go on a mission.

The elders wrote me weekly from South Dakota, bearing their testimonies of missionary work and its importance. Each letter left me feeling more empty and hopeless. There was no way I could fulfill my desire to serve a full-time mission, because I was black.

A few of the young men I'd grown really close to at Brigham Young University were preparing for their missions. Seeing their joy each time one of them received his mission call made my heart ache to receive a similar call. One of them, Craig Hall, asked me to speak at his farewell as part of the family. That was the most difficult talk I ever gave. I recall asking Craig in my talk to "please serve for two, for you and for me, because I can't go myself."

It was difficult to sing the closing hymn through my tears.

There's surely somewhere a lowly place
In earth's harvest fields so wide,
Where I may labor through life's short day
For Jesus, the Crucified;
So trusting my all to thy tender care,
And knowing thou lovest me,
I'll do thy will with a heart sincere;
I'll be what you want me to be.

(Hymns, no. 75)

"Father in heaven," I silently prayed, "will you ever have need of me?"

As my emptiness grew, so did my restlessness. I wasn't content any longer in the things I had once enjoyed. I went to my bishop and shared with him my desire to serve a full-time mission. He listened and tried his best to comfort me, then set up an appointment for me with the stake president.

President Jae Ballif listened to the desire of my heart and told me he would discuss it with the Brethren in Salt Lake City. Our meeting was on Thursday. He was to meet with the

Brethren on the very next day, Friday afternoon. President Ballif and I decided to fast that Friday, but I started my fast the moment I walked out of his office.

That Friday night I didn't hear from President Ballif, so early Saturday morning I called him. He apologized for not having called me. He had gotten back from Salt Lake City rather late. I immediately asked him what the Brethren had said. He asked if he could see me in his office on the BYU campus on Sunday afternoon. From the sound of his voice I knew that the answer from the Brethren had been "no." Hoping I was wrong, I continued fasting until my meeting with him.

When President Ballif opened his office door that Sunday afternoon, there were tears in his eyes. His first words to me were, "Mary, let's kneel in prayer." By the time he finished praying, tears were streaming down both our faces. As I sobbed uncontrollably, President Ballif held me like Daddy had when I left home to go to South Dakota. I honestly felt that he understood the pain I was going through.

From that day on I went through the motions of living, but the gnawing pain of wanting to serve a mission and not being able to do so was with me constantly. Nothing else seemed to matter. It was during this time that the Lord brought me strength through a very special brother named David Richards. He had served a mission, and we often sat talking for long hours. He would tell me about his mission and then I would try to imagine myself in his place. Though David knew of my desire to serve and often said, "Your time will come, Mary," I'm sure both of us knew it probably never would.

After a period of time I again approached President Ballif about a mission. This time I fasted and wrote a letter with

my testimony of the gospel of Jesus Christ and why I desired
to serve a full-time mission for him. I asked President Ballif
once again to ask the Brethren in Salt Lake City if I could
serve now. The answer that came back was the same — "The
time is not yet." No one, except my Father in heaven, will
ever be able to know how I hurt during that time. All I wanted
to do was to go forth, but because of the color of my skin, I
had to wait.

Don't misunderstand me. I hurt at being rejected for a
mission, but I never once failed to accept the will of the Lord.
I knew, as Elder Sekona had once told me, that all things
would eventually work for my own good. I learned during that
difficult time what patience was all about.

Time passed, and each day I had less hope that I would
ever be able to serve a mission. Each session of general conference found me listening to every word; I kept hoping and
praying that the prophet would say, "The time has come," but
after each conference, I felt more depressed and unhappy.

I was called to be the stake mission secretary. I learned a
lot about mission work and the correlation efforts needed to
help the full-time missionaries carry forth the Lord's work. The
brothers in the stake mission presidency were wonderful to
work with. All had served missions, and I enjoyed hearing the
many different things that had happened to them while they
served.

Jon Newman was from Oklahoma, and we often talked
about the attitudes of people in the South and about our
home life. Barry Ellsworth was the stake mission president,
and he shared with me some of the difficulties he had had to
overcome in his life. I in turn shared with him some of mine.
Barry had a natural sensitivity to people. One evening as he
and I sat talking he told me, with tears in his eyes, how he

had taken so much for granted, especially his priesthood. Then he said, "Mary, I know how much you want to serve our Father in heaven, and I'd give anything, even my life, if it would make it possible for you to serve that mission."

On May 28, 1978, I asked again if I could go on a mission. The answer was "no," and though I had expected it, the news still hurt as much as it had before.

My persistence — when I knew that blacks couldn't go — may seem strange, but shortly after I had been baptized, I had gone to a seminary teacher in South Dakota and shared with him my troubled feelings about the priesthood and my overall feelings of worthlessness in not being able to serve my Father in heaven to the fullest. I asked him why the Lord had blessed me to have the gospel in my life knowing it would hurt not having the full blessings. I felt the Lord was being a respecter of persons. The teacher remained silent most of the time; in fact, at that time he offered very few words of comfort.

Later that evening he asked to talk to me. He told me that the Lord had greatly impressed upon his mind words of comfort to give me in a blessing. I was to prepare myself to teach His children. He said that I would be faced with many great obstacles to build the testimony glowing in my heart. I'll never forget the last words of that blessing: "Sister Mary, the time will come when you will enter into a covenant with the Lord to go forth upon this earth and serve a full-time mission for him. Be faithful, keep his commandments, and you will see great blessings poured upon you as you live this mortal life."

I looked at that teacher afterwards and asked how that could possibly be true. He appeared pretty shaken by what he had just finished saying because, rather nervously, he shook his head and said, "I don't know. That's between you and the Lord." Without another word he walked away.

After I had been a member for about a year another interesting thing happened that contributed to my persistence in requesting a mission call. Just before Patriarch Kimball gave me my patriarchal blessing, he studied me with a puzzled look on his face and then said, "Young lady, I feel strongly impressed to tell you that if there is something you greatly desire that is not said at this time in this blessing, write it on the back of your blessing and it will become binding, depending upon your faithfulness." The day I received my blessing in the mail, I wrote on the back of it, "Heavenly Father, please bless me to serve a full-time mission to my brothers and sisters upon this earth."

Then too, there was the time I was given a blessing by Clark V. Johnson, a professor of religion at Brigham Young University. I had been asked to speak at a morningside devotional at Orem High School; feeling inadequate, I went to Brother Johnson and asked him if he would give me a blessing. His words to me were, "Mary, be strong, be faithful to the gospel of Jesus Christ and the desire of your heart will be granted unto you." There was no question that the desire of my heart was to serve a full-time mission.

These blessings were what kept me asking. Though I was slowly losing hope that I would ever be blessed to serve a mission, I felt something was going to happen. I wrote to a friend who was in Germany on a mission about the restless feelings I was having. I wrote that I didn't feel I would be in Utah the following year. I wasn't sure where I would be going, but I wasn't worried because wherever it might be it would be the Lord's doing.

On June 8 that same year I was playing in a coed softball game with my BYU ward when one of the players from the opposing team walked over to me between innings. He asked if it was hard. I thought he was referring to first-basing. I laughed and said no, I really loved it. He laughed and explained that he was talking about my people and the priesthood. Very quietly I told him yes, it was hard, very hard, especially when all I wanted to do was to serve my Father in heaven to the fullest, but the color of my skin prevented that. "It is hard," I said, "but I have centered my life on accepting my Father's will and praying that when I fail to understand, he will grant me understanding." He looked at me and said, "Someday, someday I *know* your people will have the priesthood. It probably won't be during our lifetime, but I *know* it's going to come." As he walked away I stared after him. My eyes slowly filled with tears. "If you only knew how desperately I want it to come during my lifetime so I can serve a full-time mission," I murmured. "O that I were an angel, and could have the wish of mine heart, that I might go forth and speak with the trump of God, . . . that perhaps I may be an instrument in the hands of God to bring some soul to repentance." (Alma 29:1, 9.)

The very next day the Lord opened the way. I will always remember June 9, 1978. I will always cherish the memory of the reaction of the Saints around me. Not only did I feel the heavens rejoicing, but I saw and heard the Saints around me doing the same. That special feeling radiated in the air.

I first heard the news in the employment office in downtown Provo. Bishop Bush, bishop of the ward I had been in when I came to Provo, came up to me and asked if I remembered him. He told me that he had some news that was going to change my whole life. I looked up at him, puzzled, and asked what it was.

"Your people have just been given the blessing of the priesthood."

"Please don't joke with me about something like that."

At that instant a young man who had been talking on the phone stood up and, with his fists stretched above his head, shouted, "All right!" Cold chills went completely through my body. All I could say was, "I don't believe it's happened." An older man beside me kept repeating, "I'll be darned, I'll be darned."

As I walked outside, crying like a happy kid at Christmastime, horns were honking like crazy. I stopped for a red light and a car pulled up. The driver asked me if I had heard what he had just heard. I half mumbled and half nodded a disbelieving yes. He whooped and started blowing his horn as he drove off. When I arrived at my apartment my roommates ran out to meet me, and we jumped up and down screaming with joy. Finally we went inside and each said a prayer, sobs punctuating every one.

That night I offered more thanks for the blessing that Father in heaven had added to my life that day. Throughout that night I awakened and stared at the BYU newspaper headlines, "Blacks Get Priesthood." I kept praying that I wasn't dreaming.

I wanted my family to share in this excitement with me. I had hoped they would call me after the priesthood revelation, but they didn't. A week later I finally called them. My brother Curtis answered the phone. He had to say hello twice before I found the courage to say anything. "Curtis, this is Frances." (My family calls me Frances.) He hung up. I stood there for a moment wondering what to do. I knew in my heart I was going to be hurt, yet I couldn't give up. I redialed the number, hoping Mama would answer this time. Curtis answered again. "Please just give me one . . ." Again he hung up. Feeling deeply hurt, I went to my room, curled up like a baby in her mother's womb, and cried. "How long, Heavenly Father—how long will my family keep hating me? Please touch their hearts."

The joy of my people receiving the priesthood was not only ignored by my family, but was also dulled by the realization that not all people shared my excitement. I was shocked when I saw a full-page advertisement in the Salt Lake *Tribune* declaring why my people should not have been given the blessing of the priesthood.

For days after reading that advertisement my heart was troubled. How could I reach those who felt disturbed because my people had received the priesthood and help them understand what our Father in heaven had done? I couldn't understand their feelings; after all, Father hadn't taken any blessings away from them. Did they truly know that we were all brothers and sisters? If they did, why be disturbed when a particular group in the eternal relationship finally receives a blessing others have had from birth? Finally I wrote the following letter to the man who had signed the advertisement.

July 31, 1978

Dear Brother _____ :

I read with much concern your advertisement of July 23, 1978, to concerned Latter-day Saints. As a "concerned" black I would like to respond to your ad and express a few of the "sisterly" feelings I have for you and those "concerned" Latter-day Saints who may share your views.

May I ask you to please consider the following questions:

1.   Do you believe in revelation? Was it not Joseph
Smith who gave the Church this Article of Faith as
one of its most basic premises: "We believe all that
God has revealed, all that he does now reveal, and we
believe that He will *yet* reveal many *great* and
important things pertaining to the Kingdom of God"?

2.   Do you believe in a living prophet? Did not
God tell the Old Testament prophet Amos that "surely
the Lord God will do nothing, but he revealeth his
secret unto his servants the prophets"? (Amos 3:7.)

If you truly espouse to carry a strong testimony of
the restored gospel of Jesus Christ, or in other
words if you consider yourself to be the "wheat" and
not the "tare" that grows freely in the same field,
you will most certainly answer the above questions
with a resounding yes.

As "concerned" Latter-day Saints your question is
not whether or not the blacks should hold the priesthood in light of personal interpretation to the Pearl of
Great Price scriptures, but rather is this truly the
Lord's church and does he still administer his affairs
through a living prophet. Either President Kimball is
a prophet and receives revelation from the Lord to
direct His church, or the LDS church does not
represent the Lord's true church here on the earth.

The Lord has said: "What I the Lord have spoken,
I have spoken, and I excuse not myself; and though
the heavens and the earth pass away, my word shall
not pass away, but shall all be fulfilled, whether by
mine own voice or by the voice of my servants, it is
the same." (D&C 1:38.)

Surely you must be aware that every prophet from

Joseph Smith to the present has prophesied that a day would come when the blessings of the priesthood would be extended to all people, including the blacks.

Certainly I for one never expected to see this prophecy fulfilled in my day or even in a yet future generation. No one was more surprised nor skeptical than myself. Only after much fasting and prayer did the Holy Ghost reveal to me that truly this was a revelation from God in fulfillment of that promised day.

Those Latter-day Saints who have done as I have done surely know of that which I speak and have no reason to look beyond the revelation and invent reasons to satisfy their own lack of faith and understanding.

I wonder how many "concerned" Latter-day Saints would have joined in the condemnation of the Savior nearly two thousand years ago due to a similar lack of understanding of scripture and spiritual ignorance of the revelations.

I am not condemning you nor defending myself because I am black. I just want you to realize that I, too, am a child of God and yearn to receive all the blessings you have always been entitled to because your ancestral lines go back to Father Abraham. I hope you realize and can truly appreciate this blessing, which was yours by right of birth.

If the situation were reversed, my heart would be overwhelmed with joy for you — simply because of my great love of the gospel and all the blessings it brings into my life. Does not this same happiness and

joy make you desire to share it with all people? If
it were not so, we would not be a missionary church.
For the gospel of Jesus Christ is to *every* nation,
kindred, tongue, and people.

Let me say that I would be the first to stand by you
to extend my love, support, and strength, because
you are my brothers and sisters, children of a loving
Father in heaven, who sees us for what we are inside
and not the color of our skin.

I believe in God and know that he lives. I believe in
revelation. I believe in a living prophet, and I know
of a surety that Spencer W. Kimball is truly a prophet
of God. And I know that this church is true.

I did not seek this knowledge; rather, some *really*
"concerned" Latter-day Saints sent two of their
missionaries to my door to share with me, a black, the
true gospel of Jesus Christ. They carefully taught
me the beautiful plan of exaltation and gave my life
new purpose, hope, and happiness. A wonderful
thing happened as the Spirit silently bore testimony
to my heart of the truthfulness of these things. I
rejoiced in this knowledge and believed all these things
for many years before the recent revelation given to
President Kimball.

Please, please, do not let your minds become
clouded or so confused that you lose sight of that
eternal goal to return to our Father in heaven in both
glory and exaltation, there to dwell with him forever.

Again, the Lord has said: "For my thoughts are not
your thoughts, neither are your ways my ways, saith
the Lord. For as the heavens are higher than the
earth, so are my ways higher than your ways, and my

thoughts than your thoughts." (Isaiah 55:8-9.)

May I say to you "concerned" Latter-day Saints that as children of our Father in heaven, you ought maybe to check home before you put your thoughts and ways above his.

Your sister,

Mary Sturlaugson
A truly concerned Latter-day
Saint

8

I'll Go Where You
Want Me to Go, But Not . . .

Within a month following the news of the priesthood revelation, my mission paperwork was initiated. As I completed my dental and physical examinations, I had to ask myself often if it were really happening to me. Was I really going on a mission? I didn't know how to express my thanks to Heavenly Father for the blessing of the priesthood and the opportunity of serving a mission, so I set aside a few days to fast. It was a very special time. The Lord sustained me all through my fast. I could not have endured it on my own strength. Afterwards I felt the Lord had been cheated. I had been the one who gained from the fast.

I mailed my completed papers to President Kimball on a Monday. Then waiting and wondering began. Where did the

Lord want me to serve him? The excitement grew with each passing day. I thought of places I wanted to serve, especially Africa.

On the following Friday, four days later, a friend picked me up to go shopping with him. After shopping we spent the remainder of the afternoon with his family, and later we spent time in the canyon talking. Toward late evening we started back for his home. Jokingly I said, "Let's go by my apartment so I can see where I'm going on my mission." My friend laughed and said, "Come on, Mary, you know your call hasn't come this quickly."

"Sure it has," I said, though I too knew it wasn't possible for it to be back so soon. Most mission calls took at least one month after the papers were mailed in.

When we arrived at my apartment, one of my room-mates told me I had a letter on my bed from the Church headquarters in Salt Lake City. I glanced at my friend. "Guess I didn't fill out my papers correctly." I went to the bedroom to get the letter and walked back into the living room to open it. Quickly I opened the envelope and skimmed through the letter to see where I would be going. The words jumped out at me. TEXAS SAN ANTONIO MISSION. I dropped the letter on the floor and walked slowly into my bedroom. My heart ached with disappointment. I didn't want to go to Texas. No way! I fell to my knees and cried, "Heavenly Father, please don't send me to Texas. Please don't." I knelt and pleaded with the Lord with every fiber within me. I argued, "I know I said I'd go where you wanted me to go, but there are exceptions, and Texas is one of them. I'm sorry, Heavenly Father. I want to serve a mission, but not in Texas."

Early the next week I received a "welcome to the mission" letter from President Vaughn J. Featherstone of the

Texas San Antonio Mission, along with other instructions to prepare me for the mission field. My heart felt no joyous response at all — only fear. Somehow I had to get my mission call changed.

I wrote President Kimball an extra note to mail with my acceptance letter. It read: "President Kimball, will you please petition the Lord and find out what his second choice was? Surely he doesn't want me to go to Texas. Please tell him I'll accept his second choice if it's not Mississippi."

I didn't send him that note, but I did tell him in my acceptance letter that if he was sure Texas was where the Lord wanted me, I would go, but I was afraid. I knew the attitude of whites toward blacks down there, and I honestly didn't want to go there.

Summer school at BYU served somewhat to take my mind off having to go to Texas. Most of the time I walked around with a strange feeling inside. In one of my classes that summer I met Kevin Anderson, and little by little he tried to help me see the importance of my call to Texas. He helped me realize that the Lord knew better than I where I would do the most good in his service.

One night Kevin told me about his mission and the hardships he had had. He told me I would have my share of rough times, but it would all be worth it. "Use those rough times to grow — to grow in those areas where you need growth, letting them bring you ever closer to the Savior," he said. "Mary, you'll never have this opportunity to serve the Lord in this manner again. Don't miss out on the blessing and joy of being in the service of your God by regretting where you've been called to serve. Where you've been called to serve is choice. Only you, at this time, can accomplish what the Lord needs to be accomplished. Don't fail him."

As Kevin talked, I realized the truth in what he was

saying. Daddy had been right when he had once called me selfish. I hadn't been thinking about the souls of my brothers and sisters, but only of myself and what I wanted. "Be grateful for this calling, Mary," Kevin continued. "Remember, out of all the people of your race, the Lord chose you to go forth into Texas. He called you because he knew that no matter where he called you, you would go and serve him the way he wants you to."

I honestly tried to be happy about my mission call, but the fear inside me overshadowed all other feelings. I tried letting my gratitude for being blessed to serve overcome the fear, but nothing seemed to work. Nights were miserable. I had nightmares of things happening to me in Texas. I had never known such fear.

A few weeks before I was to leave I went to my bishop. I asked him what would happen if I decided to get married instead of going on a mission. He didn't say a word for a moment. Then he looked at me and said, "Mary, the Lord needs you to serve this mission for him. If you do, and do it with all your heart, all else will fall into place and your blessings will be tenfold."

I left the bishop's office with mixed emotions. How I needed the Lord's comfort and assurance that all would be well for me in Texas! It seemed no matter how hard I pleaded for his peace, he wasn't giving it. Or was he? Maybe my fear overpowered that too.

On September 8, I went through the Provo Temple for my endowments. I woke up that morning as if in a dream. I still couldn't believe this was actually happening to me. Walking up to the temple that day, I felt as though hundreds of spirits were encircling me. There was such a feeling of love, it was almost overwhelming.

During the temple session I tried to concentrate on the

presentation, but my thoughts kept wandering to the full meaning of what was happening in my life. I was actually sitting in the house of the Lord. I could now be married and sealed to an eternal mate; I could do temple work for my ancestors; I could have my family sealed; my children would be able to serve missions. The full blessings of the kingdom were open to me now.

I began to cry. No more limitations. I didn't fully understand why the priesthood blessings had been denied to us by our Heavenly Father, but sitting there in the temple, with the tears flowing down my face, I kept remembering the scripture, "To every thing there is a season, and a time to every purpose under the heaven." (Ecclesiastes 3:1.) A woman next to me must have been aware of my tears, because she reached over and took my hand. I looked at her to thank her, and I saw that she too had tears in her eyes.

As the temple session neared an end, a peaceful feeling of gratitude filled my heart. I was aware of the tears of others in the celestial room, though I didn't know most of them. They came forward to hug me and express their happiness for the blessing I now had. What a joyous and beautiful day that was in my life! The only thing missing was my family. How special it would have been if they had been there sharing it with me!

The special happiness I found in the temple highlighted the days that followed. On September 17 my missionary farewell was held. That too was a very special day. It seemed as if the Lord had saved a special message to give me through each of the speakers. But what really caught my attention was mention of Mama's name. Brother Clark V. Johnson was speaking. The things he said made me cry with loneliness for Mama.

"I wrote Mary's mom a letter, just a short letter telling her how I felt about her daughter and what a good student she was. I told Mary what I had done. She said, 'Don't expect an answer.' Several days passed, and then came a single-spaced letter from her mom to me. I am going to read some parts of that letter:

Thank you for writing me about my daughter. I do worry about her, as I'm sure every mother does. I would have written to you sooner, but I wanted my little girl to type it for me. I'm not an educated mother, and my spelling and handwriting aren't good. I only have a third grade education, but I'm thankful to the good Lord for it. My people did not have the chance to go to school as my children now have.

I'm really proud of Mary. I have never told her this. None of her brothers or sisters have said it either, but she just keeps right on working, even though it all goes unspoken of. I don't know if Mary told you much about her family. I gave birth to nineteen boys and five girls. We have been poor most of our lives. As my children grew up and left home, most of them didn't finish high school or junior high.

Mary was the first to finish high school and the only one to go on to college. I feel she is a very special child to us, as well as all my children. But she is different. She is a strong girl. She has gone places so far from home but never showed any fear. I once asked her if she wasn't afraid that someone would try to harm her, but she gave me that smile that shone a light through her eyes and said, "No, Mama, there's

something inside me that won't let me fear what
I cannot see."

I'm proud of her, and you sound like a friend.
She's talked much about you. She never once said
whether you were white or black. I wanted to ask her
but I did not. She seems to have reached that point
in her life where people have no color.

I'm not well. I do not know how long the Lord will
give me on this earth but if in the near future I do not get
to tell my daughter, will you please tell her that I
was proud of her? Let her know this, will you? I see
a love for God in her that is so real. People in this
area are still talking about how warm and sweet she
was to talk to. People thought she would be snooty
because she had a college education, but they said she
acted and treated them as her equals. She let them
know that she gave thanks to God, and most young
people here are not doing that.

Pray for her, will you please? Pray that she will always
have the love and strength of God. Pray for her to
give love to the people that give not to her, and please
pray that what she was trying to tell us, we may
someday understand if it is true. I pray that God will
bless you and your family.

"In Mary's own way, she had a great influence on these
brothers and sisters," Brother Johnson continued. "None of
them are members of the Church, I don't think, as of yet, but
you can see that her mother said please pray for her and, in-
directly, pray for us that we might know that what she's doing
is true.

"Mary, in the next two years you're going to know frustration. You are going to know danger. You are going to be thrown out of more places than you ever thought possible. You'll be spit on. You'll be hot, tired, and hungry. But remember how the missionaries converted you. You said, 'No matter how mean I was, they just kept on smiling and smiling and smiling.' You just keep that smile your mother talked about, that smile that lights up your eyes, and you'll be a success. 'If you labor all your days and bring save it be one soul unto me, great shall be your reward.' I think that with her personality, with her liveliness, her impishness, her mischievousness, all of which make her a fun person, if she can transfer these to the mission field and receive the special blessings that come to those set apart and called, Mary will be a great missionary."

I don't remember what else Brother Johnson said because all I kept thinking was, *Mama loves me.*

President Clare Bishop, the mission president at the time of my conversion, spoke. He told me plainly why I had been called to Texas.

"It has been said many times in the Church that the Lord raised a special generation of young people. If that is the case, surely Mary must be a special spirit among these special spirits. When I think of Mary and her conversion, I think of the parable of the sower. Two young missionaries were in South Dakota sowing seeds. Some seeds fell into rich deep soil, hard-crusted at first. But as they tilled and truth was found, Mary joined the Church. She has withstood the thorns that have tried to grow and choke her out. But there is another part to that parable, an unwritten part. Mary is now to be the sower. As a missionary, sowing seeds, Mary will be sorely tempted. As one of the first black missionaries, her temptation will perhaps be different. I had an occasion the other day, with the assignment committee, to find out why Mary was being sent to Texas, and the message came loud and clear. 'Mary is a child of God. She is sent out among the children of God, and she is to teach the children of God, whoever they are and wherever they might be found.' With this comes great responsibility, but the Lord knows that Mary is the one who can accomplish the work that needs to be done in Texas."

As I stepped forward to give my talk, my heart felt lighter than it had in months. I had had very little release from an agonizing depression since my call to Texas. But as I stood up to speak, I felt a warm feeling and the Spirit bearing witness to me that my call was divine and from God, and he was now — and always would be — beside me. I fought the tears as I tried hard to express what was in my heart.

"I really don't know where to begin to tell you how I feel. There is much in my heart. I have told Heavenly Father how afraid I am to be going to Texas and that I am afraid that he might go away and leave me alone as my family has. But no matter how many times I tell him I feel this way, the peace and reassuring answer always come back the same. 'I am with you always.' I still wonder if that goes for Texas too.

"Last night I asked the Lord one last time if he had made a mistake in calling me to Texas. I don't want to go there. I'm afraid of how I will be treated. I'm afraid of seeing and feeling the hatred and rejection I saw and felt as a child. I'm afraid of how the whites will treat me, not because of the message I have to share or the church I represent, but simply because of the color of my skin. It's a frightening feeling, and I feel so weak.

"I promised the Lord that I would be willing to go wherever he wanted me, but I never thought he would take my 'wherever' to mean Texas too. I tried convincing the Lord last night to wait until he got some big black football player and send him to Texas. I do have to marvel that he wants me to go there. I told a friend the other day that I just knew I wouldn't come back, and he said. 'Sure you will. You'll come back in a pine box.' I love that kind of encouragement!"

Toward the end of my talk I felt again an assurance of my calling, and grateful that no matter what happened to me, I would be happy for the choice calling I had been given and the place where I would labor in "earth's harvest fields so wide."

9

With Heart, Might, Mind, and Strength

On September 28, 1978, I entered the Texas San Antonio Mission field. Before leaving I made five definite promises to the Lord:

I told him how much I loved and missed my family and promised that I was going to leave them in his care. I would serve him with all my heart.

I promised him I would serve him with every ounce of energy I had and with all my might.

I promised him I would eat, drink, sleep, and think the gospel that I was called to share. Thus I promised him my total mind.

I promised him I would endure to the very end no matter what the people in Texas did to me. I promised him all my strength.

I didn't know what I would encounter in the mission field,

so last of all, when trials came my way I promised to remember the beautiful examples of four special people:

Doug, the one white boy in my high school senior class. I would remember the persecution Doug had gone through when he really didn't have to.

Elder Sekona, the missionary who had brought me the gospel. I would remember the love and patience he had with me and how in tune he had been with the Lord so he would know His will and not give up until that will had been accomplished.

Mama. I would remember Mama's faith in the Lord. I would strive to have that same faith. Mama also has love — love she gives freely when it isn't returned. Mama is kind and always wants to do things for others. She has joy; no matter what happens to her, she is always happy, always looking for the good and finding it.

My Brother, the Lord and Savior Jesus Christ. I would remember Doctrine and Covenants 122:7-8: "And if thou shouldst be cast into the pit, or into the hands of murderers, and the sentence of death passed upon thee; if thou be cast into the deep; if the billowing surge conspire against thee; if fierce winds become thine enemy; if the heavens gather blackness, and all the elements combine to hedge up the way; and above all, if the very jaws of hell shall gape open the mouth wide after thee, know thou, my son, that all these things shall give thee experience, and shall be for thy good. The Son of Man hath descended below them all."

All the way to Texas I felt as though I were dreaming, and often I questioned if all this was really happening to me, Mary Frances Sturlaugson. The joy in my heart was totally inexpressible.

And now here I am on the plane returning to Salt Lake

City. Eighteen of the greatest months of my mortal life have
raced by me and it's over long before I've wanted it to end.
Months have seemed like days, and a year and a half like only
a few short months. As I sit on the plane, my head leaning
against the seat, I try to relive every experience. Some
memories bring pain; some, fear; and some, laughter. . . .

My arrival in Texas had been on the news programs
there, and as we went from door to door people recognized
me. "Oh, you're the one I saw on TV." Then they wanted
to know why I'd become a Mormon. My companion and I
used these times to bear our testimonies. There were those
who opened their doors, pointed an accusing finger, and said,
"You're a Mormon?" Often people laughed, then slammed
the door. One old gentleman looked shocked and angry as
he said, "You mean to tell me there are 'niggers' in the
Mormon church too?" I simply learned to smile and not show
the hurt that dug so deeply into my heart.

The hurtful and discouraging times got so bad that one
night I decided to call my family hoping to find love and
encouragement there, but all I found was more hurt and discouragement. The news report about my going on a mission
had been shown in Tennessee, too, and my family was very
angry. They told me that now the whole town knew I was a
cotton-picking (my translation of the actual words used)
Mormon. I don't know which of my brothers it was, but one
of them yelled into the phone that he wished I was dead. I
hung up the phone, went into the kitchen, and cried hope-
lessly. I prayed for my family to forgive me for the pain I was
causing them. As I prayed, my brother's words echoed
through my mind — "I wish you were dead."

Five months after my arrival in Texas, I was called to

serve in one of the roughest areas of the mission—an area where rapings were frequent and involved little girls five years of age as well as women in their late sixties. If a day passed without killings it was history. People broke into homes there just for a hobby. Sister missionaries had never served in this area, and for some reason the Lord chose my companion and me to be the first set of sisters to go there. As we rode toward the area I kept asking myself if the Lord was trying to get rid of me.

It was in this area that my companion and I tracted out a woman who at first was extremely reluctant to allow us into her home. On our second visit to her house we discovered the cause of her reluctance. She was a member of the Ku Klux Klan and sometimes acted as the secretary for them. Her husband had been a prime organizer for the local Klan chapter and had vowed that no "nigger" would ever set foot inside his house. But her heart had been touched, and despite many heart-breaking obstacles, she continued to grow in the gospel and was, with her husband's permission, baptized into the Church. After her baptism and confirmation she presented me with a gift. I unfolded a T-shirt that said "Secret Member of the Ku Klux Klan." Everyone laughed, including me.

That rough area turned out to be a "gold mine" of people waiting to hear the gospel, and we found ourselves constantly running short of time to handle our many appointments. We were dubbed "Starsky and Hutch" because of the way we raced frantically from one appointment to the next.

One morning while hurrying to reach an appointment on time I hit a parked car. A week later we were stopped by a military policeman who was all set to give us six citations: speeding, no Texas license, a broken headlight, a broken windshield (a result of the previous week's accident), no post sticker, and a sixth I can't recall. We knew we were guilty on all counts, so we did the only thing left to do — we asked him the golden questions. We invited him to church and a week later he was baptized. We never did get those six citations!

. . . The "fasten your seatbelts" sign is flashing. Thoughts of my mission are cut off abruptly. Oh, there are so many more experiences I want to cling to, to savor just a little longer, but the plane is beginning its descent. I feel uncertain, especially when I turn my thoughts from my mission to my future. My family will not be meeting me nor do I have a "home" to return to. Will there be anyone at the airport to meet me?

I feel lost and alone. I can almost hear Mama singing a song she sang to us as children, "Sometimes I feel like a motherless child, a long, long way from home." Mama always cried as she sang this song. Once I asked her why, because she was at home. All Mama said as the tears fell was, "Child, someday yous will know, yous will know."

I wait for the plane doors to open. Silently I pray. *It's really happening, isn't it, Heavenly Father? I've really left the mission field.*

I step into Utah's mountain air. Many hands begin waving to me, and my heart wells with gratitude for the love I see on the faces of those who have come to meet me. I move forward confidently, another prayer in my heart.

"What now, Lord?"